Profitable Bible Study

By

WILBUR M. SMITH

SECOND REVISED EDITION

BAKER BOOK HOUSE
Grand Rapids, Michigan

Copyright © 1963 by Baker Book House Company
First printing, November, 1971
Second printing, November 1973
ISBN: 0-8010-7943-8
Library of Congress Card Catalog Number: 62-20932

Printed in the United States of America

To my dear Father

THOMAS SYLVESTER SMITH

MERCHANT

Given to Hospitality

Member of the Executive Committee of
the Board of Trustees of the
Moody Bible Institute

Elder of Moody Memorial Church
for the last quarter of a century

Who, like Job of old, has, since they were born,
risen early every morning to
plead with God for his children
And who has walked uprightly
before us all these
forty years

With deepest love and gratitude

Just about a quarter of a century ago, late in the year 1938, I placed in the hands of the W. A. Wilde Company, a manuscript which was published in 1939 as *Profitable Bible Study*. The first half of the book was devoted to eight methods for studying the Scriptures, and the second half to what the subtitle announced as "An annotated list of the first one hundred best books for the Bible student's library." Two most gratifying results followed the publication of this volume. In the first place, it would seem from letters I have received through the years, and from oral communications as well, that some hundreds of ministers and missionaries began to build their libraries around this classified list of books. In fact, the book itself proved in one way somewhat of a nuisance to dealers in second-hand theological books, because so many ministers came in with a list of books they did not have, taken from this suggested bibliography. My list did not confine itself to recently published volumes, but included a number that had appeared around the middle of the nineteenth century, and had become very, very scarce, such as the volumes by Candlish on the First Epistle of John. So, as a second result, publishers became aware that some of these out-of-print books might well be brought back into print, so that since this volume first appeared, I would say that at least forty of the volumes that were then out-of-print, have been made available again, including the Candlish volume; the great work of Krummacher: *The Suffering Saviour*; the two volumes on the Atonement by Smeaton; Liddon's masterly *Explanatory Analysis of St. Paul's Epistle to the Romans,* etc., etc.

In 1951, a new edition was called for, which gave me the opportunity of thoroughly revising the bibliography. Now, a quarter of a century after this volume first appeared, a third edition is called for, and I have again completely revised the list of suggested books.

What a vast amount of literature pertaining to the Scriptures has appeared since 1939, and some of it of the very first quality! Actually, there are more books appearing annually relating directly to the interpretation of the Scriptures, than any one minister, or professor, can find time for reading, and this necessitates exercising some discrimination in determining what one will read and what one must pass by. Thus, for example, during the last ten years, sixteen new *series* of commentaries on the Bible have been launched— some series have been completed, as the *Abingdon Commentary,* while others are still in process of publication. Seven new Bible Atlases have appeared in the last nine years, and the most important one-volume Bible Dictionary of the twentieth century has just been published. Since the first edition of *Profitable Bible Study,* the Dead Sea Scrolls were discovered, around which a whole library of literature has been written; and the State of Israel has been established, where literally hundreds of books about the Bible are being published every year. Due to the publication of the Revised Standard Version, we now have a shelf of new books, some of them quite important, relating to the history of the English versions of the Bible. Two new Reference Bibles have been published within the last twelve months, and two more are to appear before the end of 1964.

There has been a tremendous upsurge of interest in Bible study throughout the Western world during the last two years. The Roman Catholic Church has never published so many important books on the Bible as in this generation. More emphasis is being placed on the study of the English Bible in many of our Seminaries. Correspondence courses pertaining to the Scriptures are now available in a score of languages for missionaries, some of them with phenomenal results as in the countries of North Africa. The instability and threat of world conditions in this atomic age has aroused new interest in the prophetic Scriptures. This is a pre-eminently important hour for Biblical study, and for the teaching of the Word of God, and those engaged in this work have never had so much truly helpful, well-written, dependable material to work with as in this decade.

What is now really needed is a comprehensive bibliography covering all the principal subjects relating to the Bible and the history of the Christian church, such as Bishop John Fletcher Hurst produced in 1896, in his still valuable *Literature of Theology*. I still have hopes of producing such a work myself during the next two or three years, providing someone else does not anticipate me in this.

CONTENTS

Profitable Bible Study

INTRODUCTION

The Need Among Young Christians for Systematic, Devotional Bible Study

G<small>REAT</small> multitudes of young people, from summer to summer, are attending Bible Conferences and Young People's Conferences all over the country. They hear stirring messages; hundreds here begin their Christian life; thousands come away quickened and renewed in their spiritual experience. They hear it continually emphasized that Bible study is of paramount importance in maintaining a strong Christian life; they resolve in their own hearts that in the days to come they are going to study systematically and regularly the Word of God, and live in the power which such study communicates. They put these resolutions into practice immediately when they get home. For one reason or another, however, many of these young people do not seem to get out of their Bible study what they had expected: perhaps they do not know what to look for in their study of the Bible; or do not know how to obtain definite results from such study; or do not understand what they are reading; or other things continually interfere and interrupt such study. It is

7

not long (though they would not confess it) before they experience a dullness in it all, and their resolutions are soon broken. Bible study then becomes intermittent, and increasingly unsatisfactory, until, perhaps three or four months after coming home from a summer Bible Conference, it is entirely discontinued. The young Christian knows he has been defeated. Perhaps some sin comes into his life, and he knows that the cessation of Bible study is at the root of the whole tragedy. His testimony grows cold, his enthusiasm for the work of the Lord wanes, and he naturally becomes discouraged.

Now there is absolute deliverance from all this defeat in the study of the Bible. There *is* a way of approaching the Word of God, of beginning to study its inexhaustible contents, which, instead of dulling with us, will continually increase our enthusiasm for Bible study, and hold us with an ever firmer grip, until the habit becomes absolutely settled in our lives, and we are finding the results so great and noticeable that not for anything would we ever give it up. This article is written particularly with young people in mind, with the hope that it might, in a very simple way, teach them some of the more profitable methods of studying the Word of God.

All that follows is written, not from a theoretical standpoint, but from a practical one. This book does not pretend so much to tell young people what they *ought* to do, as what they *can* do. It is not written for ministers, or experienced Sunday School teachers, or for those who are students at Bible Institutes. There is not one person of high school age but who can employ every method of Bible study suggested in this elementary treatment of the subject. What is written here is the result of personal experience. Much that the author might have said fifteen years ago he does not dare to say now, by which he means that he today more truly realizes the limitations of time among our young people, the weakness of human flesh, and all the many, many influences which might lead a young Christian (and older ones, too) away from such a study. He simply wants to face this whole question in a very simple, and he trusts, helpful way, so that no young person can say: " I just do not know *how* to study the Bible. I want to do it, but I don't seem to be able to find a way for doing it."

This book is not written to tell young men and young women how to master the Bible for an examination in some college course, or how to become great teachers of the Word of God, or how to write a book about the Bible, or even how to prepare messages for Young People's Meetings. It is not meant to be technical in any way. What we need first of all is the Word of God nourishing our own souls. We need spiritual strength, victory over sin, joy in our daily experience, a love for souls, a passion for the Lord Jesus, and power in our testimony. As an outstanding leader of young people said at Northfield forty years ago: " How shall we study the Bible? I should like to say at the very outset that no man can answer that question for another man. He can devise a method of Bible study which he may wish to commend to others, but the only Bible study that is of any large value to a man is the Bible study that meets his own personal needs; and just as his own personal needs differ from the personal needs of every other man, the method of

Bible study which will be best for him will probably be best for him alone." Continually throughout this treatment the author is thinking, not so much of an intellectual grasp of the historical and geographical contents of the Word, as he is of a spiritual apprehension of the Word of God, and appropriating of its teachings in our own hearts and souls. The title of this book carries in it the purpose of the author— " How to Study the Bible for the Enrichment of the Spiritual Life."

Making Up Our   Before we give careful attention to
Minds That We   the question of *how* we may study
Are Going to   the Word of God for our spiritual
Study the Bible   enrichment, we shall perhaps do
  well to consider for a moment *why*
we should make Bible study pre-eminent in our daily lives. Is it not true that many do not regularly and earnestly study the Word of God because they have never really become convinced that such study is *indispensable?* Some months ago, a very dear friend of the author's, a man about sixty years of age, was running up the steps of Broad Street Station, Philadelphia, carrying two heavy suitcases. The man weighed two hundred and forty pounds. Before he got to the top of the steps, his heart almost gave out. This man is a doctor. He said instantly this thought came into his mind: " You will *have* to take off some of this weight." He began taking it off the next day. He has taken off forty-five pounds, and weighs less today than he has for thirty years. Of course he has no more trouble with his heart. He told me that he found the greatest battle was, not the taking off of the weight,

but *coming to a conclusion that that weight must come off.* Once he had decided that he *would* take it off, the battle was over, and there was no further conflict in his mind over the matter. Now, if we could come to an hour in our lives when before God we would say that Bible study *must* be given a definite, paramount place in our lives, every day, because we realize that we *absolutely need it,* then, no matter what interruptions are experienced, or what might be our immediate reactions to such study, we would keep at it persistently, because we knew we *needed* it. Let us think, then, for just a moment, of our absolute need for the Word of God as Christians.

I. Seven Great Things the Study of the Bible Will Do for Us

1. *Discovers and Convicts Us of Sin* For many years British journals regularly carried a large advertisement of a famous institution near London, known as the Sandow Institute, where those whose health had been broken by disease or worry could recover their strength, and return again to work and the normal duties of life. It is probable that thousands of Britishers have been actually restored to robust health by the Sandow treatment. Now the world, our own flesh, and Satan himself together work for our spiritual weakening and the breaking down of the very tissues of our souls, so that thousands of Christians live an ænemic existence, spiritually speaking, without power, or joy, or vision, or fruitfulness in their lives. It is one of the great purposes of the Word of God to deliver Christians from such invalidism, to restore to them the power, the glow, and the fruitfulness that Christ intended they should possess when He redeemed them.

There were four definite steps in the Sandow treatment (and in any similar treatment)—a diagnosis of the trouble; a removal of whatever was causing the trouble, poison, the pressure of some bone upon a nerve, or whatever else it might be; a carefully prescribed diet; and exercise. Now the Word of God does just these four things for us. First, *it diagnoses our case*. In Hebrews 4: 12, the Word of God is spoken of as " a discerner of the thoughts and intents of the heart." The Greek word here translated " discerner " is the word *kritikos*, from which is derived our English word " critic." As a professor of English literature criticizes a composition which we submit to him, that he might point out to us its errors and blemishes, so that they might be removed, and tells us wherein the manuscript might be improved, so God, in His Word, is the supreme and final critic of our lives. The Apostle Paul in his last Epistle (2 Tim. 3: 16) tells us that the Holy Scriptures are profitable " for conviction," by which he means they are able to convict us of our sins, revealing the dark spots in our lives against the background of God's holiness. The Apostle James (1: 23, 24) tells us that the Word of God is as a glass, a mirror into which we look, discovering the blemishes upon our countenances, the stains which the world has left there. Just as a man cannot see his own face except in a mirror, so a Christian cannot see the spiritual and moral blemishes of his life except as he looks into the Word of God. In

1 John 1: 9 we are told that: " If we confess our sins,
He (God) is faithful and just to forgive us our sins,
and to cleanse us from all unrighteousness." The word
here translated " confess " is the Greek word *omologeo*,
consisting of two words, *omo*, meaning " the same,
identical," and *logeo*, meaning " to say, to speak."
Thus, the word " confess " literally means " to say the
same thing as another, to agree with, to consent to."
The word gives a picture of two people talking. They
are in disagreement about a certain matter, but, as
they continue to discuss the matter, whatever it might
be, the arguments and evidence presented by one con-
vinces the other that he is wrong. Thus they finally
agree. When we confess our sins, we are saying the
same thing that God says about us. God points out
in His Word what sin is, and, when we confess sin to
God, we admit the existence of some iniquity in our
lives. We would never know sin except it were revealed to us by God, and, when we keep away persistently from the Word of God, we become callous
and indifferent to the sins of our lives. In the pointed
words of Izaak Walton—

> " Every hour
> I read you kills a sin,
> Or lets a virtue in
> To fight against it."

John Calvin could testify, out of a life of incessant
study and profound scholarship, in his *Institutes of
the Christian Religion:* " No human writings, however
sacredly composed, are at all capable of affecting us in
a similar way. Read Demosthenes or Cicero, read

Plato or Aristotle, or any other of that class. You will, I admit, feel wonderfully allured, pleased, moved, enchanted; but turn from them to the reading of the Sacred Volume, and whether or not it will so affect you, so pierce your heart, so work its way into your very marrow that the comparison of the impression so produced, that of orators and philosophers, will disappear, making it manifest that in the Sacred Volume there is a truth Divine, something that makes it superior to all the gifts and graces attainable by man." Centuries later, another famous student of the Word of God, whose Reference Bible has been such a blessing to millions of Christians throughout the English world, Dr. C. I. Scofield, made the following confession: " I gave much of my earlier life to the study of Homer and Shakespeare, and while my understanding undoubtedly profited by that study, and I found keen intellectual delight in it, these books held no rebuke for my sins, nor any power to lift me above them, but, when I came to the Bible and received Him, concerning Whom, after all, the whole Book is written, I entered into peace, joy, and power. The Bible led me to Jesus and Jesus transformed my life."

2. Cleanses Us from the Pollutions of Sin   After sin is detected and confessed, we need *our lives cleansed from sin's pollution*. This is exactly what the words in 1 John 1: 9 promise us: if we confess sin, God will " cleanse us from all unrighteousness." The word here translated " cleanse " means nothing less than " to free from the defilement of sin, to purify from wickedness." Hundreds of years before this, the Psalmist had grasped the same important truth when he wrote: " Wherewithal shall a young man *cleanse* his way? by taking heed thereto according to Thy Word " (Psalm 119: 9). On the way to the Garden of Gethsemane, on the night of His betrayal, our Lord said to His disciples: " Now are ye *clean* through the Word which I have spoken unto you " (John 15: 3). Again, in the Garden, in that wonderful prayer which He offered to His Father in pleading for His followers, He asked God to " *sanctify* them through Thy Word: Thy Word is truth " (John 17: 17). The idea is repeated by the Apostle Paul in his Ephesian letter: " Christ also loved the Church and gave Himself for it; that He might *sanctify* and *cleanse* it with the washing of water by the Word " (Eph. 5: 25, 26). We do not know how the Word of God cleanses us, but we do know that it *does* cleanse us.

The story is told of an English woman engaged in washing some clothes which she held in a large aluminum sieve at a river bank. She was approached by a Church of England clergyman, who had preached in her village about ten years before, and she, recognizing the minister, fervently said to him: " Oh, sir, I remember when you were here many years ago. I heard you preach and your sermon cleansed my soul." " What was my text that day, Madam? " asked the clergyman. " Oh, I could not recall what the text was. I haven't been able to remember it for years." " Well, then, if you cannot even remember the text, how can you say that my sermon cleansed your soul? " " Well," said the woman, " you see this water pouring through this sieve washing the dirt out of these clothes that are held by the sieve. So the word of your text did not remain in my soul, but the Word of God, passing through my soul, cleansed it of its impurities." The author has never seen this particular power of the Word of God to cleanse carefully expounded by any Biblical expositor, but he does want to bear his own personal testimony to the truth of it. More than once has he felt the cleansing, purifying power of the water of God's truth carrying away the impurities deposited in the soul by life in the world.

3. *Imparts* The Christian needs conviction, needs a
Strength detection of his sin, a diagnosis of his case, and a confession of sin first—nothing of any importance can take place in his spiritual life until that takes place. But even after sin is confessed, and put away, and the heart is cleansed from it, the Christian needs something else—he needs *food for new strength*. As impurity in the blood means a weakening of one's physical strength, often accompanied by exhausting fever, so sin in the life of the Christian results in weariness, weakness, fatigue, and an inability to do the work God has called us to do. The Word of God is given to us for just this purpose—to communicate new strength to our weakened lives.

There is a beautiful picture in the Old Testament which aptly illustrates man's need for strength, and God's provision for that need. You are familiar with the record of the Passover, in Exodus 12, wherein the Lord commanded that a lamb, without blemish, should be slain, and that the blood of that lamb should be struck upon the two side posts and on the upper door post of each house. "For," said the Lord, "I will pass through the land of Egypt this night, and will smite all the first born in the land of Egypt, . . . and the blood shall be to you for a token upon the houses where ye are: and when I see the blood, I will pass over you, and the plague shall not be upon you to destroy you, when I smite the land of Egypt." Now we all know that the slain lamb and its blood is a type, a symbol of the coming Lord Jesus Christ, the Lamb of God Who shed His blood for the sin of the world. But there is another striking picture in this chapter. After Israel was ordered to kill the lamb, they were told: " And they shall eat the flesh in that night, roast with fire. . . . And thus shall ye eat of it; with your loins girded, your shoes on your feet, and your staff in your hand; and ye shall eat it in haste: it is the Lord's Passover." It was the shed blood of the lamb, struck upon the door posts, that *saved* the eldest male in each family, but Israel was about to embark upon a wilderness journey, and it was necessary that they have *strength* for their pilgrimage. *And the food by which that strength was provided was the lamb which had been slain.* What a thrilling comparison we have here with Christian experience. Every believer is *saved* by the shed blood of the Lord Jesus Christ, but the believer is a stranger and a pilgrim (Heb. 11: 13) until he shall be with his Lord, and it is necessary that he *feed on the Lamb in order to have strength for this earthly pilgrimage.* The Lamb is the Word of God (John 1: 1); the living Word, the Lord Jesus Christ; and the written Word, the Bible. For strength, we *must* feed on Him and on His Word.

Early in Israel's history God said: " Man shall not live by bread alone, but by every word that proceedeth

out of the mouth of God " (Deut. 8: 3)—the very
words that our Lord used when resisting the temptation of Satan in the wilderness (Matt. 4: 4). Twice
the Psalmist likens the Word of God to honey (19: 10;
119: 103). Job testified: "I have treasured up the
words of His mouth more than my necessary food "
(Job 23: 12). Jeremiah could say: "Thy words were
found, and I did eat them; and Thy Word was unto
me the joy and rejoicing of my heart " (Jer. 15: 16;
see also Ezek. 2: 8–3: 3; Rev. 10: 9, 10). Three times
in the New Testament the Scriptures are referred to
as milk (1 Pet. 2: 2; 1 Cor. 3: 2; Heb. 5: 12, 13);
once they are compared to meat (Heb. 5: 12, 14).
Because of the power of the Word of God to communicate strength, Paul could say to the Ephesian
elders: "And now, brethren, I commend you to the
word of His grace, which is able *to build you up* "
(Acts 20: 32; see also 2 Tim. 4: 1–4). The Apostle
John, writing at the close of a long life of devotion to
Christ and of glorious victory over sin in a world
antagonistic to God, wrote—" I have written unto you,
young men, because ye are strong, and the Word of
God abideth in you, and ye have overcome the wicked
one " (1 John 2: 14). Would you pardon me if I
called your attention to some wonderful words of Dr.
Alexander Maclaren on this last verse—they are so
much better than anything I could write, and they
ought to be read and pondered by all of us, often.

" Let me say to you, then, if you want to be strong,
let Scripture truth occupy and fill and be always present to your mind. There are powers to rule and to
direct all conduct, motive powers of the strongest
character in these great truths of God's revelation.

They are meant to influence a man in all his doings, and it is for us to bring the greatest and solemnest of them to bear on the smallest things of daily life. Suppose, now, that you go to your work, and some little difficulty starts up in your path, or some trivial annoyance ruffles your temper, or some lurking temptation is suddenly sprung upon you. Suppose your mind and heart were saturated with God's truth, with the great thoughts of His being, of His love, of His righteousness, of Christ's death for you, of Christ's presence with you, of Christ's guardianship over you, of Christ's present will that you should walk in His ways of the bright hopes of the future,—do you think it would be possible for you to fall into sin, to yield to temptation, to be annoyed by any irritation or bother, or overweighted by any duty? No! Whosoever lives with the thoughts that God has given us in His Word familiar to his mind and within easy reach of his hand, has therein an armlet against all possible temptation, a test that will unveil the hidden corruption in the sweetest seductions, and a calming power that will keep his heart still and collected in the midst of agitations. If the Word of God dwell in your hearts, the fangs are taken out of the serpent. If you drink any deadly thing it shall not hurt you, and you will ' be strong in the Lord and in the power of His might.'

" Notice that remarkable phrase, ' Ye have overcome the wicked one.' He is talking to young Christians before whom the battle may seem to lie, and yet He speaks of their conquest as an accomplished fact, and as a thing behind them. What does that mean? It means this, that if you will take service in Christ's army, and by His grace resolve to be His faithful soldier till your life's end, that act of faith, which enrolls you as His, is itself the victory which guarantees, if it be continued, the whole conquest in time. Whosoever has exercised, however imperfectly and feebly, the faith in Jesus Christ the Lord has therein conquered the Devil and all his works, and Satan is henceforth a beaten Satan, and the battle, in essence, is completed even in the act of its being begun. What a priceless thing it is that you may begin your independent manhood with a conquest that will draw after it ultimate and supreme victory."

4. *Instructs Us in What We Are to Do* With our case diagnosed, the trouble discovered which is causing us such suffering and weakness in our Christian lives; with our souls cleansed of all impurities and stains; with each day finding us partaking eagerly of the Word of God for new strength, we need one more thing—*exercise, i.e.,* putting into practice what we have found in the Word of God, or, in other words, using the strength which we have derived from eating the Word, in doing the things the Word commands us to do. It should be carefully noted in the remarkable picture of the two men which our Lord drew for us at the end of His Sermon on the Mount that *both* of these men had *heard* the Word of God, but the one who built his house on the sand had not *obeyed* the Word which he had heard; whereas the one who built his house upon the rock is the one who actually *did* what the Lord had commanded him to do (Matt. 7:24–27). There are many Christians born again, with Christ in their hearts, and with some knowledge of the Word of God, who, nevertheless, are unfruitful in their lives, without power, without victory, because they are not doing what the Word of God has so clearly told them to do. Let it be recognized at once that one cannot advance far in the study of the Word of God if he is going to throw up a screen of disobedience behind which he lives. So the Apostle James admonishes us that we are to be " *doers* of the Word, and not hearers only, deceiving your own selves " (James 1: 22).

5. *Provides Us with a Sword for Victory over Sin* Changing from our figure of the Sandow Institute, we might mention three other reasons why we *must* determine in our lives that, no matter what else happens, we *will* constantly, regularly, sincerely study the Word of God. As he drew toward the end of his wonderful message to the Christians at Ephesus, the Apostle Paul reminded them that they would have to stand against the wiles (or the stratagems) of the Devil, and that this great conflict would take place, for many of them, " in *the* evil day," *i.e.*, in a day fearfully characterized by evil, when the thought of the world would be evil, when the books that were read would be evil, when the very teachings of some schools of learning would be evil, when men would be practicing evil and rejoicing in it. How many young people know what that is today! And when he gave to the Ephesians the secret for victory in such a time, he commanded them " to take the sword of the Spirit which is the Word of God " (Eph. 6: 17). Here is a weapon which will never fail in defeating our great arch-enemy, Satan, and in giving us *the power to stand against every evil force.* Our Lord so used it. Millions of Christians down through the ages have found it absolutely dependable. We need it supremely in these last days for victory over the Evil One. We can only wield the sword of the Spirit as we carry the Word continually in our hearts, wherein is the field of battle. We can only consider ourselves soldiers truly equipped with the sword of the Spirit when we have incorporated that Word in our lives, when we not only believe the Bible as a whole, but when we have taken into our lives some of its promises, and are living, by faith, in the power which it can give. Is not this what the Psalmist meant when he said: " Thy Word have I hid in mine heart, that I might not sin against Thee " (Psalm 119: 11)?

If you have read Bunyan's immortal classic, *The Pilgrim's Progress,* you will remember the vivid account he gives of Christian in the Valley of Humiliation. It is worth repeating. " Poor Christian was hard put to it. For he had gone but a little way before he espied a foul fiend coming over the field to meet him; his name was Apollyon. Then did Christian draw, for he saw it was time to bestir him; Apollyon as fast made at him, throwing darts as thick as hail. . . . The sword combat lasted for about half a day, even till Christian was almost quite spent; for you must know that Christian, by reason of his wounds, must needs grow weaker and weaker. Then Apollyon, espying his opportunity, began to gather up close to Christian, and wrestling with him gave him a dreadful fall; and with that Christian's sword flew out of his hand. Then said Apollyon, ' I am sure of thee now.' And with that he had almost pressed him to death, so that Christian began to despair of life. But as God would have it, while Apollyon was fetching his last blow, thereby to make a full end of this good man, Christian nimbly reached out his hand for his sword, saying, ' Rejoice not against me, oh mine enemy: when I fall I shall arise '; and with that gave him a deadly thrust which made him give back as one that had received his mortal wound. Christian perceiving that made at him again, saying, ' Nay, in all these things we are more than conquerors through Him that loved us.' And with that Apollyon spread forth his broken wings, and sped him away, so that Christian saw him no more. . . . I never saw Christian all this while give as much as one pleasant look, till he perceived he had wounded Apollyon with his two-edged sword; then indeed he did smile and look upward. . . . Then there came to him a man with some of the leaves of the tree of life, the which Christian took and applied to the wounds that he had received in the battle and was healed immediately."

6. *Makes Our Lives Fruitful* Another reason for being regular students of the Word of God is found at the opening of the Psalter: " Blessed is the man that walketh not in the counsel of the ungodly, nor standeth in the way of sinners, nor sitteth in the seat of the scornful. But his delight is in the law of the Lord; and in His law doth he meditate day and night. And he shall be like a tree planted by the rivers of water, that bringeth forth his fruit in his season; his leaf also shall not wither; and whatsoever he doeth shall prosper " (Psalm 1: 1–3). These words are to be placed alongside of the remarkable promise which God gave to Joshua after the death of Moses. "This book of the law shall not depart out of thy mouth; but thou shalt meditate therein day and night, that thou mayest observe to do according to all that is written therein; for then thou shalt make thy way prosperous, and then thou shalt have good success. Have not I commanded thee? Be strong and of good courage; be not afraid, neither be thou dismayed: for the Lord thy God is with thee whithersoever thou goest" (Joshua 1: 8, 9). Think of it—the efforts of our lives guaranteed to be always fruitful! The beautiful things of life are not to fade ever. In whatever we undertake in the name of the Lord we will succeed. We need never know discouragement. The Lord will be ever at our side!—providing we meditate continually upon the Holy Scriptures and "do according to all that is written therein."

7. *Gives Us Power to Pray* There are many other reasons we can give for making Bible study paramount in our Christian lives, but we take time to mention only one more, a promise which our Lord gave when He was here on earth: "If ye abide in Me, and My words abide in you, ye shall ask what ye will, and it shall be done unto you" (John 15: 7). Power in prayer! The right to approach God in absolute confidence that what we ask for in His will He will give us. The more His words abide in us, the more our prayers will be in accordance with His will. How wonderful if all of our needs, all of our longings, all of our hopes, were prompted only by the Word of God, and then all that we ask for we would know that we would receive. What influence we could wield! What strength would be ours! What work would be accomplished! What lives would be redeemed, if every day we were pleading at the Throne of Grace in the power of the indwelling Word of God!

In writing his last letter, the Apostle Paul reminded Timothy that " in the last days perilous times should come," but he knew of something powerful enough to give to Timothy, and to give to any other Christian in any day of peril, absolute victory in his own life, and abounding fruitfulness—the Word of God. " But continue thou in the things which thou hast learned and hast been assured of, knowing of whom thou hast learned them; and that from a child thou hast known the holy Scriptures, which are able to make thee wise unto salvation through faith which is in Christ Jesus. All Scripture is given by inspiration of God, and is profitable for doctrine, for reproof, for correction, for instruction in righteousness: that the man of God may be perfect, throughly furnished unto all good works " (2 Tim. 3: 14–17). This is what we want, that we may be men and women of God, complete in our lives, thoroughly equipped for every work that God calls us to do. This we may be, this we will have, if we abide in, lay hold of by faith, incorporate into our lives, and put into practice the Divine teachings of the Word of God.

The late Professor C. Alphonso Smith, in his fascinating little book, *What Can Literature Do for Me?* gives to his six chapters the following headings:

I. Give You an Outlet.
II. Keep Before You the Vision of the Ideal.
III. Give You a Better Knowledge of Human Nature.

IV. Restore the Past to You.

V. Show You the Glory of the Commonplace.

VI. Give You the Mastery of Your Own Language.

These are all very commendable things. Literature certainly has its place in our lives. But how infinitely greater are the results of studying the Word of God for us—it gives us a knowledge of our own sinfulness, provides a perfect cleansing from every stain, restores to us the power and strength which sin took away from us, equips us with a weapon by which our greatest enemy can be defeated, promises us success and fruitfulness in our own Christian lives, enables us to pray with prevailing power at the Throne of Grace, instructs us in truths which we could never elsewhere discover,—the truth of God, the truth of salvation through Jesus Christ, the truth of eternal life, the truth of a home in Heaven; empowers us that we might adequately, enthusiastically, courageously do God's work here on earth as long as He chooses to leave us in this world.

II. Eight Methods for Studying the Bible for Our Own Soul's Nourishment

1. *Should We* We are now ready to talk together
Study the about some of the methods by which
Bible a Book we can get out of the Bible its richest
at a Time? treasures for our own spiritual nourishment. I said in the first chapter of this study that this book would be of a very practical nature, and that it would be written out of

my own experience. This will compel me to say something at this point that contradicts a rule laid down by most Bible teachers when they are discussing methods of Bible study. Again and again I have come upon statements by Bible teachers in which they earnestly plead with Christians to study their Bibles by books, *i.e.*, to master one book of the Bible at a time, to read a book of the Bible at one sitting, to get its general outline, direction, purpose, and its fundamental teachings. It is granted that this is a wonderful way for studying the Word of God. Its results are exceedingly rich; but I think, personally, that it is too much to ask of young Christians, to read through one book at one sitting, and to attempt to get such a grasp of it that they will be able, in one reading, to discover for themselves the great fundamental teachings of the book, its construction, development, and paramount purpose. What we need is *daily* food for our souls, and, if a young person should begin to read, for example, the Gospel of Matthew, with the purpose of mastering the main outlines of the book, he would either have to give it at least two consecutive hours, and most young people will not take that much time every day (and cannot) for Bible study, or he will read in the book for a period of twenty or thirty minutes, taking almost the entire week to read the book through, and, when he has finished, the book does not hang together in his mind because his reading of it has been broken up into so many separated periods. When he gets to the end of the week he has read the Gospel of Matthew through, but the material is so abundant that his mind, rather than seeing the Gospel as a whole, is probably more or less filled with a multitude of ideas, and the result is more or less chaos for him. What I am pleading for is not a method of Bible study that will make one a great teacher of the Word, or prepare one to pass an examination; but a method whereby one can have *daily* food and nourishment from the Word. For this reason I do not commend the reading of the Bible by books for one's devotional study of the Scriptures. This method has a fundamental place, but that place is in the study, where one is attempting to gain an intellectual comprehension of the Scriptures, rather than in the oratory where one would approach God and have God draw nigh to him. This will somewhat surprise many, perhaps, and provoke a little controversy, but I can only speak of what I myself think is practical, and not what other Bible teachers commend. I have never seen, myself, among all the young people I have known, any one who could really show definite results after having attempted to study the Bible in such big sections.

2. *Studying the Bible by Chapters* Most chapters of the Bible are just long enough for a morning period of devotion. In fact, one wonders whether or not the Spirit of God, when He led Cardinal Hugo to divide the Bible into chapters, did not have this very thing in mind, that thus would Christians be enabled the more easily to feed daily upon easily apprehended sections of the Word. It is, however, one thing to *read* a chapter of the Bible: it is another thing to get something out of it for your own soul. Let me be very practical now. I would suggest, in fact, I would urge, with the greatest earnestness, that when you read a chapter, you do not

conclude your study of it until you have discovered an outline for the chapter, however simple that outline might be. Almost all chapters in the Bible, either in whole or in part, have within them a definite development, and it is in discovering that development that we find their richest spiritual teachings. Let us take one or two illustrations.

The opening chapter of the book of Joshua naturally breaks into three parts:

I. The Word of God to Joshua (vv. 1–9).

II. The Word of God through Joshua to the Israelites (vv. 10–15).

III. The Israelites Declare Their Allegiance to Joshua (vv. 16–18).

Here is a leader who does not speak to the people he is to lead until God has first spoken to him (notice the little word *then* in verse 10). When God has spoken to this leader, he can go before his people with courage, conviction, and assurance. When the people behold a leader to whom God has spoken, they are ready to follow his leading. How we need just this very truth today in the lives of all of us who are called to be leaders in Christian work!

Turn over a few pages until you come to the fifteenth chapter of First Samuel, and you will find four steps leading down to the hour of Saul's tragic rejection:

I. Saul is Commanded of God to Slay the Amalekites (vv. 1–6).

II. Saul Refuses to Obey Completely God's Command (vv. 7–9) (notice the little word *but* with which the ninth verse begins).

III. The Discovery of Saul's Sin and Its Denunciation (vv. 10–25).

Here is a remarkable illustration of what we were speaking of in a preceding paragraph of the power of the Word of God to convict of sin. " Then came the word of the Lord . . . and Saul said unto Samuel, I have sinned " (vv. 10, 24).

IV. God's Rejection of Saul as King (vv. 26–35).

How many Christians, knowing the Word of God, called to a great work for God, have, nevertheless, because they disobeyed God, been rejected for such great work, thereafter knowing a life of ineffectiveness and consequent grief! What a warning!

Many a young Christian, in beginning a regular devotional study of the Word of God, will turn to the first book of the New Testament and, of course, to the first chapter. A young Christian, when he first reads this chapter, might be tempted to believe it could not give him any particular soul nourishment, yet, unless one has success at the very beginning of his Bible study, he will soon become discouraged and give it up. I would say that we ought never to leave a chapter until we have really seen in it, or in a large section of it, a development of some theme. If a chapter does not have at least one great truth for us upon our first reading it, then we ought to read it over again. If the time has gone for our devotional reading on any one day before the chapter has yielded some truth for our souls, then we can give it further thought while riding down to work on the street car, or walking to work, or as we go about the house in the normal duties of every day; and often by night-time, we will find the chapter yielding some rich truth for our souls. If necessary, go back to the chapter the next day, or take the next chapter for a change, and then go back to the earlier chapter a day or so afterwards, but *do not let that particular passage in the Word remain for you a barren area:* keep drilling through the soil and rock until you strike Living Water. My own experience has been that a chapter which involved the most thought, and which at first refused to give me anything, finally yielded up some spiritual teaching of unusual richness.

In the biography of Mary Slessor of Calabar we are told that her own reading of the Bible was done early in the morning as soon as there was light, generally about 5: 30, when " she took a fine pen and her Bible and turned to the book she was studying in the Old or the New Testament. She underlined the governing words and sentences as she went along in her endeavor to grasp the meaning of the writer and the course of his argument. . . . Sometimes it would be three days before she would leave a chapter, but she did not leave it until she had some kind of idea as to its purpose. She was her own commentator, and, on the margin, she noted the truths she had learned, the lessons she had received, her opinions about the sentiment expressed, or the character described. When one Bible was finished, she began another and repeated the process, for she found that new thoughts came as the years went by."

But we must look at the first chapter of Matthew, of which we were speaking. It breaks naturally into four parts, all of them with Christ as their subject:

I. The Royal Ancestry of Jesus Christ (vv. 1–17).
II. The Miraculous Conception of Jesus Christ by the Holy Spirit (vv. 18, 19).
III. The Annunciation of the Advent of Christ by the Angel of the Lord (vv. 20, 21).
IV. The Fulfillment of Prophecy by the Coming of the Lord Jesus Christ (vv. 22–25).

No other being that ever lived, or that ever will be born on earth, could be the subject of such a chapter as this, with a royal ancestry, conceived by the Holy Spirit, announced by an angel from Heaven, and fulfilling prophecy by His coming! Thus the first chapter in the New Testament lifts the subject of the whole Bible, the Lord Jesus, far above every other person ever born on earth. Finding this truth, we lift our souls in adoration and worship, grateful for Him Who cometh from above and is above all.

Every chapter in the Bible will not be quite as rich as these we have referred to, though hundreds of them will be, and some chapters can be found with even richer teaching than that which we have discovered in these three, but *there is no chapter anywhere in the Bible but that will yield some spiritual teaching.* There are 1189 chapters in the Old and New Testaments, enough for devotional reading for over three years, if we should take a chapter every day. Miss Grace Saxe suggests the following ten questions which we may ask of each chapter:

   I. What is the principal subject of this chapter?
  II. What is the leading lesson of this chapter?
 III. Which is the best verse in this chapter?
  IV. Who are the principal persons in this chapter?
   V. What does the chapter teach concerning Christ?
  VI. Is there, in this chapter, any example for me to follow?
 VII. Is there, in this chapter, any error for me to avoid?
VIII. Is there, in this chapter, any duty for me to perform?
  IX. Is there, in this chapter, any promise for me to claim?
   X. Is there, in this chapter, any prayer for me to echo?

What depths, what power, what Christ-likeness, would our lives know, if we just simply followed this one method of studying the Word of God for our souls' profit, beginning with the first chapter of Genesis and continuing until we had finished the last chapter of Revelation!

But remember that we are not bound by rules, nor are we slaves to any method, and, when we have studied one book of the Bible, chapter by chapter, it might be well to turn to some other method of Bible study for a change, and then come back to the chapter method at a later period.

3. *Studying* Often in a chapter one will come upon
the Bible by a particular portion, frequently printed
Paragraphs in the Revised Version as a single paragraph, that will give one an abundance
of material for his own soul for a morning's meditation,
or for five or six devotional studies. Each of the parables and the miracles in the Gospels might be considered as such. The conversations that our Lord had
with the many people with whom He came in contact,
as recorded in the four Gospels, might also be considered as paragraph passages for devotional study.
Every prayer in the Bible, and every single important
event, might be considered specifically as paragraph
passages. Not every one will be interested in each
paragraph of every chapter. At one period of our lives
we might not be drawn at all to the study of a certain
passage in the Bible, when, some years later, that very
passage might prove to us one of the sweetest, richest
portions of God's Word. Our needs, the things which
immediately interest us, our circumstances, our work,
our ages, will often determine what paragraphs will
yield the greatest results in our study. Each one must
determine this for himself. We will take one simple
illustration from the fourth chapter of Acts, verses
23–31, an account of the wonderful prayer meeting
held in the Jerusalem Church shortly after the Ascension of our Lord. The occasion for this prayer meeting
will be found in the preceding verses. The ultimate
results of the prayer meeting will be found in the
succeeding verses. We devote ourselves now to the
paragraph dealing with the prayer meeting itself,
discovering in its rich sentences five primary facts relating to prayer:

I. Why This Particular Prayer Was Offered:
"And when they heard that, they lifted up their voice to God."

It was the report of the Apostles concerning their treatment by the chief priests and elders that led to this prayer, just as often in our lives persecution, difficulties, and opposition drive us to the Throne of Grace.

II. The Manner of Their Praying.

In verse 24 we are told that they "lifted up their voice to God with one accord," *i.e.*, with perfect harmony. Our Lord said: "If two of you shall *agree* on earth as touching anything that they shall ask, it shall be done for them of My Father Who is in Heaven" (Matt. 18: 19). These early Christians were together in mind and heart, in longing, faith, and hope. Moreover, if you will take the trouble to look up the word here translated "prayed" (in verse 31) in a large Bible Concordance, you will find that the original here is the Greek word *deomai,* and you will also find that this same word is often used by Luke in his recording of the fervent pleading of men who besought the Lord urgently for one thing or another (Luke 5: 12; 8: 28; 9: 38; 22: 32). These people were *laying hold of God with fervor,* they were pleading with Him, they were insistent in their prayers, not letting God go until they were assured of an answer.

III. The One to Whom Prayer Was Offered.

The One to Whom these people prayed was the Lord God, the Creator, the Omniscient One (because He knew hundreds of years before

Christ was born the antagonism of the rulers against His Son), the Father of the Lord Jesus, the One Who determines beforehand all the acts of men. What prayer would mean to all of us if in our praying we were conscious of God possessing all the greatness, majesty, and power that were ascribed to Him by these early Christians!

IV. The Requests Made in Prayer.

These men on their knees asked for only three things: that the Lord would look on the threatenings of the Jewish high priests, elders, and officers; that they themselves, the disciples, might speak the Word of God with all boldness; and that God, by His power, through the Name of Jesus, might grant signs and wonders to be done in the early Church.

V. The Immediate Consequences of This Prayer.

There were three immediate results—the place was shaken, they were all filled with the Holy Spirit, they spoke the Word of God with boldness. There is enough here to feed our souls for days, to deepen the life of prayer, to renew our vision, to quicken our faith, to restore hope, all this from just nine verses of Scripture.

We might take one other simple paragraph—almost the last words of the Apostle Paul (2 Tim. 4: 9–13). Here Paul asks for three things: for Timothy himself to come, for the cloak that he left at Troas, and for the books and parchments. Paul has a body—it must be kept warm; he has a mind which he wants to keep occupied with reading the finest things obtainable; he has a heart, and, in the midst of an awful prison, where pagan criminals surrounded him, he longs for one whom he loved. How human this all makes the Apostle! How close we feel to him! Further illustrations are not needed. They could be multiplied by the hundreds.

4. Studying the Bible by Verses When we begin to use individual verses for our devotional study, we come into a field of unlimited possibilities and of inexhaustible wealth. It is not easy to tell a person how to study a particular verse of the Bible because verses differ so much one from another. Some are concerned with historical matters, some with doctrinal matters, some are narration, others are exposition, and others are descriptive. No set rules can be laid down which will give us the key to the study of every verse in the Bible. One might do well, in looking at a verse, to take out all the verbs and arrange them in order, as, *e.g.*, such a simple sentence as Romans 8: 28: "And we know that all things work together for good to them that love God, to them who are the called according to His purpose." Here are four verbs—*know, work together, love,* and *are.* These are all in the present tense. Three of them have reference to Christian believers; one of them refers to all the circumstances of life. Then one might discover in this verse what is said about God: on the one hand, we have been called according to His purpose; on the other hand, our love is poured out toward God. His purpose toward us precedes our affection toward Him. One might consider the points of time in this verse: our calling is in the past, our love for God is that which we have now. The good toward which all things ultimately work will often be in the future; all things do not work together today because all things are not known or in force today, but, when the suffering of today is followed with the results of that suffering tomorrow, when the disappointment of today is followed by the unexpected joy of tomorrow, then *all things* have worked together for our ultimate good. Finally, we should remember that this verse is not a warning, it is not an admonition, it is hardly a promise; it is a statement of fact, and, as such, coming from God, is to be received by faith.

The words of the great scholar and translator of the Scriptures, John Wycliffe (1324–1384) could hardly be improved upon when we are thinking of the study of the great verses of the Bible.

> " It shall greatly helpe ye to
>   understande Scripture,
>   If thou mark
>   Not only what is spoken or wrytten,
>   But of whom,
>   And to whom,
>   With what words,
>   At what time,
>   Where,
>   To what intent,
>   With what circumstances,
>   Considering what goeth before
>   And what followeth."

Some verses are so brief they will not lend themselves to outline, while others can be divided in a most marvelous way. Take, *e.g.*, that precious verse, John 3: 16. It may be divided in many ways, among which the following is one:

I. The Ultimate Source of Our Salvation—God's Love.

II. The One Through Whom Salvation Is Mediated —God's Only Begotten Son.

III. Our Part in Participating in the Salvation God Has Provided—Believing in God's Son.

IV. The Consequences of Receiving the Salvation God Has Provided—Everlasting Life.

Or take such a sentence as Galatians 1: 4: "Who gave Himself for our sins, that He might deliver us out of this present evil world, according to the will of our God and Father." Here we find at least three great truths:

I. God Our Father Has a Will, a Plan, a Purpose for Us.

II. That Purpose Is That We Shall Be Delivered from This Present Evil Age.

III. To Accomplish This in Us the Lord Jesus Christ Gave Himself Up for Our Sins.

Whenever you and I come to the place where we long for deliverance from any besetting evil and the power of temptation, we can rest in this, that before we desired such deliverance, God had desired just that for us, and, moreover, the Lord Jesus Christ has died to make that deliverance possible and real in our lives! With a verse like this in our minds we can go singing to our work and face fearlessly the world that is about us.

While reading the Epistle of Jude in the Revised Version not long ago, I came upon a verse, or rather, a part of a verse, that just filled my heart with joy for weeks after. I think it was the most thrilling experience I had during a whole month of my vacation, just to find this clause: "To them that are called, beloved in God the Father, and kept for Jesus Christ" (Jude 1). It is God Who calls us, God Who loves us, and God Who will keep us. If He calls us and loves us, surely He will keep us. If He keeps us, no one can take us away from Him. But we are kept, not alone that we ourselves might have peace and joy, but that we might glorify Christ here, and glorify Him in the glory to come. I discovered, and any reader of an English Concordance can discover the same thing, that the verb here translated "kept" is the same one used with reference to the guards who kept the tomb in which Jesus was buried (Matt. 28:4), and the same one used in referring to the centurion who kept the Apostle Paul (Acts 24:23). It is also the same verb which our Lord Jesus used when He asked His Father in Heaven to keep, through His own Name, from all evil, those whom God had given Him (John 17:11–15). It is the verb used by Paul when he spoke of our whole spirit, soul, and body being *preserved* entire at the coming of our Lord Jesus Christ (1 Thess. 5:23). This is the verb which is used by our Lord when He gave the promise, "I will keep thee" (Rev. 3:10). When a verse like this

dawns upon a believer, his whole life is suffused with
a new glow, and the whole world about him is changed,
as he looks upon it through the confidence that this
promise bestows.

There are thousands of verses in the Bible which, in
themselves, will give us all that we need for any one
devotional period.

5. *The Study* There are said to be 8674 different
of Words in Hebrew words in the Old Testament,
the Bible 5624 different Greek words in the New
Testament, and about 6000 different
English words in the entire Bible. Of course every
word in the Bible will not yield a great spiritual truth,
or refresh our hearts, and yet there are hundreds of
words in either Testament which, if really studied, will
amazingly deepen, and strengthen, and enrich our spiritual experiences. Let us confine ourselves to the word
believe, and its use in only one book for a moment,
in the Gospel of John. What a wonderful study is
thus developed! We think first of *the One in Whom
we are to believe,* God (5: 24; 12: 44), and the Lord
Jesus Christ (3: 16; 6: 29, 69; 9: 35, 36, 38; 11: 27;
12: 42). In the second place, we might think of *the
reasons for believing on Christ.* There are at least
six of them given by John: the testimony of John the
Baptist (1: 7); the Word of Christ (1: 50; 4: 41, 42;
8: 30, 31; 13: 9; 14: 29; 16: 30, 31); the miracles of
Christ (2: 11, 23; 7: 31; 10: 25, 37, 38; 11: 45); the
resurrection of Christ (20: 8, 29); the testimony of
God (5: 30–37); the unity of believers (17: 21).
Then John reveals to us *the consequences of believing:* we will have eternal life (3: 15–18; 5: 24; 6: 40,

47; 20: 31); we will never thirst (6: 35); we will never be judged (3: 18); we will accomplish great things for God (14: 12); we will not abide in darkness (12: 46); out of us will flow rivers of living water (7: 38, 39). Finally, we are told of the tragic *consequences of not believing* in the Lord Jesus—such men are condemned (3: 18); they shall not see life (3: 36); the wrath of God abideth on them (3: 36); they shall die in their sins (8: 24).

It is interesting always to note the first time some significant Biblical word occurs in the Scriptures. Take that simple verb of invitation, *Come*, and then look at its first reference—"And the Lord said unto Noah, *come* thou and all thy house into the ark" (Gen. 7: 1). Here is the key to all the invitations proceeding from God. They are invitations to shelter from storm, to accept a salvation already provided, an urgent plea to escape coming doom. There is love, earnestness, and urgency in the word.

Or take, if you will, any one of the titles of Christ. What spiritual riches await us in quietly meditating upon such titles of our Lord as the Word, the Bread, the Light, the Vine, the Door, the Son, the Saviour, the Life, the Lord, and the Lamb. Take only the first one for a moment, the *Word*. A word is an expression of an idea held in our minds, uttered not for our sakes, but for others, that they might know what we are thinking. Furthermore, what we think is only a product of what we are. We are what we think and we think as we are. If Christ is the Word of God, He is God's expression of Himself to us. Through Christ God speaks, and in Christ God is revealed. Just as one person ascertains the character of another through his words, written or spoken, so we know God as He is through the expression of Himself in Jesus Christ, the Word of God. This is what our Lord meant when He announced to the disciples: " No man hath seen God at any time; the only begotten Son, Who is in the bosom of the Father, He hath declared Him " (John 1: 18).

We can take the little word *full*, and trace it through the New Testament to discover how many things there are that ought to *fill* our lives. A study of the words " increase," " abound," and " grow," will reveal how stunted the Christian lives of some of us have become. It is most interesting to make a list of all the passages in which the word *know* occurs in the New Testament, and then let such a study be followed by each of us asking ourselves the question—" As a child of God, *do I know* what I ought to *know?* "

There is no book in the world whose words will yield such treasures of truth, such spiritual richness, such rivers of refreshing water, such strengthening of the soul as the words with which the Holy Spirit has inspired the authors of the books of our Bible. In fact, I am inclined, more and more, to believe, as my own Bible study continues, that in this *word-study* of the Scriptures we will find some of the most precious things for our souls that God desires us to have.

6. *The Fascination of Biblical Biographies*   The late Professor Alfred Cave once said: " Let a man, whatever he do, but do it greatly, especially let his greatness be seen in goodness, and we cannot help sitting at his feet to learn as well as to listen. Lives of great men, as Longfellow reminds us, bring to our remembrance the possibilities of our own lives." Dr. Douglas Southall Freeman, the writer of the monumental four-volume life of Robert E. Lee, the most important American biography of this century, has recently said: "Men read biography, I think, primarily because they live it. When they peruse history, they are onlookers, but when they study a life, they participate in it." The things which happened to the great characters of the Scriptures are recorded, as the Apostle Paul reminds us, "for our admonition" (1 Cor. 10: 11). It is estimated that there are 2930 different men and women mentioned in the Bible, though, of course, many of these are only referred to by name, and will hardly furnish enough material for a biographical study. Nevertheless, there are hundreds of characters in the Old and New Testaments, the study of which will prove as fascinating as any method of Bible study that can possibly be conceived. Without going into great detail, the author of this article would suggest the following points for examination in the study of any Biblical biography, though often it will be found that evidence on some of these points is not given in the Scriptures:

I. Collect all the material which the Bible contains concerning the one character about to be studied.

In doing so, be sure that you are not gathering material for two or more different persons of the same name, *e.g.*, there are thirty characters in the Old Testament by the name of Zechariah, there are fifteen characters in the Old Testament by the name of Jonathan, and there are twenty characters by the name of Nathan. In the New Testament we have eight characters by the name of Judas, seven women who bear the name of Mary, five different men called James, and five different men called John. It is interesting to note, however, that many of the great characters of the Bible have a name not used by any other one person in the Scriptures, *e.g.*, there was only one Abraham, one Isaac, one Jacob (in the Old Testament), one Moses, one David, one Solomon, and one Isaiah. On the other hand, it should be remembered that some men have more than one name, as, *e.g.*, Peter is called Peter, Simon, Cephas, and Bar-Jona.

II. Carefully study the ancestry of each character, and especially the characteristics of the parents, if they are known.

III. Attempt to estimate the advantages in training which the subject of your study had during the early days of his or her youth.

IV. Carefully attempt to determine the work which your character accomplished.

V. What was the great crisis in this person's life, and how did he meet it?

VI. What traits of character does this person display throughout his life?

VII. What friendships did the man have—were they noble or ignoble; did they help him or hinder him in his life work?

VIII. Determine, as far as possible, the influence

this particular character had upon others, upon the nation, upon the history of religion.

IX. What growth does the character of this person show?

X. Carefully determine the religious experiences of the character you are studying—his prayer life, faith in God, service for God, knowledge of the Scriptures, courage in testimony, and his attitude in worship.

XI. What faults and shortcomings are revealed?

XII. What do you think was the great sin in any one character's life, if there was one? What was the nature of the sin? What were the steps leading up to the sin? What effect did this sin have upon this person's future?

XIII. What do you find to be the character and influence of this person's children?

XIV. In what way do you think the character you are studying is a type or anti-type of Christ?

XV. What is the one great lesson in this person's life for you?

It might be interesting to begin a study of a certain group of characters, as, *e.g.*, the anonymous characters of the Bible, or the servants of the Bible, or the great failures of the Bible, or the friends of Jesus, or the souls which Jesus touched. As an illustration of the biographical method of Bible study, one might begin, say, with the life of Noah. Without going into all the points above, we might just consider No. XII. Noah's great sin, of course, was his getting drunk (Gen. 9: 20–25). What do you think was the cause of his drunkenness? This is an interesting point, especially in the light of present conditions in our country. As far as we know, he did not disobey any command of God when he partook of the fruit of the vine, and drank wine. He simply over-indulged himself. He lost self-control, which is the root of so many of our sins. Even things which might be innocent pleasures are abused sometimes by over-indulgence. The results were disastrous. It led his own sons to laugh at their father, and undoubtedly lowered the estimate of the father in the minds of his sons. We can easily imagine that it irreparably hurt his testimony. Whatever conclusion we may draw from it, the fact is, there is no record in the Bible that Noah was used again by the Lord. His sin is followed by three hundred and thirty years of silence.

An interesting study along this line would be, *e.g.*, the life and work of the Apostle Peter as revealed in the Book of Acts. We might suggest the following headings:

I. The events of his life in the Acts of the Apostles.

II. A summary of his work—in administering the affairs of the Church, as a preacher, as a witness to the Lord Jesus, as a worker of miracles.

III. The convictions of the Apostle Peter: about the Lord Jesus, about the Holy Spirit, about the Scriptures, about God the Father, about salvation.

IV. Peter's associations with other believers.

V. The character of Peter as revealed in the Book of Acts.

Then we might ask, in conclusion, some questions about Peter in the Book of Acts. Why does he disappear from the stage of history in chapter 15? In what way could you say that Christ's promise to Peter that he would be a rock was fulfilled in the events of his life which are here recorded? In what way did he suffer for his convictions? What encouragement is there for us in God's wonderful use of the Apostle Peter even after his terrible denial of the Lord Jesus?

Very recently, in studying the references in the Old Testament to Ethiopia, I came upon a most fascinating character, about whom really a great deal is said, but who had, I am sorry to say, heretofore entirely escaped my attention. His name is Ebedmelech. Do you know anything about this man? The record of his courageous life you will find in Jeremiah 38 and 39.

7. Learning to Pray from a Study of the Prayers of the Bible We have already said in this book that one of the results of personal Bible study would be the strengthening and deepening of our own spiritual experiences. Hardly in any way will such results be more abundantly obtained than in a careful study of the prayers of the Bible. It will be found that there are approximately eighty-three prayers in the Old Testament, and forty-nine prayers in the New Testament, of which twenty-eight are to be found in the Gospels. The following points may be considered in a study of any prayer.

I. The one who is Praying—is he or is he not a child of God?

II. The Circumstances which lead to Prayer—God's goodness will lead to thanksgiving. A new sense of God's glory and majesty will lead to adoration. A consciousness of guilt will lead to confession. A knowledge of the needs of others will lead to intercession. One's realization of one's own deep need for guidance, healing, strength, courage, food, etc., will lead to petition.

III. The Physical aspects of Praying—the time when prayer is offered, day or night; the place in which the prayer is offered, in public or in private, out-of-doors or in a church; the attitude of the body in praying: the position of the hands, kneeling, the eyes opened or closed.

IV. The Definite Word used to indicate the act of praying.
It will be a most interesting study to look up the shades of meaning for the different words translated "pray" or "prayer" in the Old and New Testaments.

V. The one to whom Prayer is offered.
Which Person of the Trinity?
What title of God is used in praying to Him?
What attributes of God are recognized in such praying?

VI. The General Order of the Prayer. The five forms of prayer are: Adoration, Thanksgiving, Confession, Petition, and Intercession.

VII. The Subject or Subjects of the Prayer.

VIII. The Relation of the Prayer to the promises of

the Word of God (see such passages as Num.
14: 17, 18; 2 Sam. 7: 27, 28; 1 Kings 8: 22–
53; Acts 4: 25, 26).

IX. The Answer to the Prayer.

Is the answer recorded or assumed from later
events? How long between the offering of the
prayer and the answer to the prayer? If an
answer is not given at once, is the prayer
offered again? (See, *e.g.*, Matt. 26: 36–45;
2 Cor. 12: 7–10.) If the petition is not
answered, is there a reason given for such
silence? (See Deuteronomy 3: 25–27.) Does
God ever answer some prayers that would be
better unanswered? (Psalm 78: 31; 2 Kings
20.)

X. The Result of the Prayer—for the one praying; for others, *e.g.*, the revival that followed
the prayer of Ezra (Ezra 10).

8. *Finding* Our Lord, in talking to the two dis-
Christ in All ciples on the Emmaus road, " beginning
the Scriptures at Moses and all the prophets, expounded unto them in all the Scriptures
the things concerning Himself " (Luke 24: 27). All the
Scriptures testify to the Lord Jesus Christ (John 5: 39).
He is God's eternal Word, and, wherever God is revealed, there may the Lord Jesus Christ be found. In the
Old Testament we may find Christ in the Theophanies
(*i.e.*, the appearances of Christ in the form of a man,
or an angel, before His incarnation, as, *e.g.*, to Abraham, Gen. 18). He may be found in the sacrificial
offerings of the Old Testament, and in the services of
the Tabernacle and the Temple. He, of course, is to

be found in the magnificent prophetic passages which predict His coming, both as a suffering Saviour, and as a reigning King. He may be found in the types of the Old Testament, especially in the typical persons there revealed, as, *e.g.*, Adam, the order of the priests, Melchizedek, Joseph, David, et cetera. But Christ is pre-eminently to be found in the New Testament. Of course we know He fills the Gospels, but how many have ever attempted to explore the inexhaustible wealth of material concerning the Lord Jesus Christ in the Book of Acts, and the Epistles of the New Testament, as well as in the Book of Revelation? Let us take for an example of such a study the revelation of Jesus Christ in the two Epistles of Peter. We may outline such a study as follows:

I. His Pre-Incarnation—foreknown indeed before the foundation of the world (1 Pet. 1: 20).

II. His Incarnation Manifested at the End of the Times (1 Pet. 1: 20).

III. The Names of the Lord Jesus.
There are 21 different names and combinations of names in these two Epistles alone, some of which never occur in any other part of the Bible, as, *e.g.*, " the Bishop of our souls " (1 Pet. 2: 25).

IV. The Life and Character of Christ.
Peter reminds us that the Lord was gracious (1 Pet. 2: 3); precious (1 Pet. 2: 4, 6); sinless (1 Pet. 2: 22; etc.); majestic (2 Pet. 1: 16).

V. His Suffering and Death.
It is amazing how many times Peter, in his

sermons in the Book of Acts, and in his two Epistles, refers to and comments upon the death of Christ. Here we are told He was rejected of men, reviled, that He suffered for sins, for us, for the unrighteous; that He died, bearing our sins in His body on the tree; that He was put to death in the flesh that He might bring us to God, that we might live unto righteousness, that we might be sprinkled by His blood and redeemed.

VI. Christ's Work Between His Death and His Resurrection.

He preached unto those in prison (1 Pet. 3: 19, 20).

VII. His Resurrection.

It was accomplished by God. It results in our being begotten again, and in our having a good conscience toward God.

VIII. His Exaltation.

He is at the right hand of God. He is made the Head of the Corner. Angels and mortals are subject unto Him. His is the glory and the dominion forever.

IX. The Second Advent of Christ.

See, *e.g.*, 1 Pet. 1: 7, 13; 4: 5; 5: 4; 2 Pet. 3: 4.

X. Our Relationship to Christ.

We are to follow in His steps (1 Pet. 2: 21); we are to sanctify Christ in our hearts (1 Pet. 3: 15); we are to grow in the grace and knowledge of our Lord and Saviour Jesus Christ (2 Pet. 3: 18).

What would it mean if we possessed a Bible with

blank pages inserted, and such can be purchased, and should make an outline, in more detail than this, of the teachings of each book in the New Testament concerning the Lord Jesus Christ, and then incorporated that teaching in our lives? Surely then we would have what the Apostle Paul so eagerly sought for himself, the very mind of Christ, knowing Him in the fellowship of His sufferings and the power of His resurrection. For " this is life eternal, that they might know Thee, the only true God, and Jesus Christ, Whom Thou hast sent " (John 17: 3).

A Few   There are innumerably more subjects for
Additional   Bible study. We have mentioned only
Suggestions   eight of them, and there is no time for
               the consideration of any more, but the
following subjects will prove of some value when one wants to enter upon a new field for his devotional study.

    I. The Words that Have Come Down to Men from Heaven.
   II. The " Fear Nots " of the Bible (about 200 passages contain this comforting phrase).
  III. The Great Conversions of the Bible.
  IV. What the Bible Has to Say About Itself.
    V. The Violations of the Ten Commandments and the Consequences of Such Disobedience.
  VI. The " Musts " of the Bible (especially those in the life of Jesus).
 VII. The Teachings of Jesus as Practiced in His Own Life.
VIII. The Attributes of God.

IX. The Gifts of God and of His Son.
(The study of the verb " give " in both Testaments will reveal nearly three hundred different gifts from God and from Christ—some to all men, some only to Christians, some to individuals, *e.g.,* thirteen specific, different gifts to David.)

X. The Questions Jesus Asked Men.

XI. What Christ Asks Us to Do for Him (*e.g.*— to follow, look, seek, believe, love, watch, feed, go, tarry, etc.).

XII. The Invitations of Jesus.

XIII. The Emotions of Jesus (*e.g.,* joy, sorrow, grief, love, compassion, etc.).

XIV. The Emotions Aroused in Others by Jesus (*e.g.,* amazement, anger, etc.).

XV. Verdicts Concerning Christ Recorded in the Gospels: *e.g.,* by Simeon (Luke 2: 30–32); by the wise men (Matt. 2: 11); by John the Baptist (John 1: 29, 34, 36); by the Samaritans (John 4: 42). How many know, *e.g.,* that Pilate gave six different verdicts regarding Christ, all of them laudatory?

XVI. The Person and Work of the Holy Spirit.
(This can be studied best by considering the subject in each separate book of the New Testament.)

XVII. The Great Revivals of the Old and New Testaments.

XVIII. The Words of Christ.

Here we might stop a moment and give our readers an example of what a rich study this last subject can be. We give the following outline, which contains enough spiritual food for a week or more:

THE WORDS OF CHRIST

I. Their Divine Origin.
    1. Foretold by God to Moses—Deut. 18: 18.
    2. Reaffirmed by John the Baptist—John 3: 34.
    3. Declared by Christ Himself—John 7: 16; 8: 28, 38; 12: 49, 50; 14: 10, 24; 17: 8, 14.

II. Their Abiding Characteristics.
    1. Eternal—Matt. 24: 35; Mark 13: 31; Luke 21: 33.
    2. Gracious—Luke 4: 22.
    3. Authoritative—Luke 4: 32.
    4. Spiritual—John 6: 63.
    5. Living—John 6: 63.
    6. Unique—John 7: 46.
    7. Wholesome—1 Tim. 1: 6.

III. Their Power in Our Hearts.
    1. To cleanse—John 15: 3.
    2. To teach us to pray effectively—John 15: 7.
    3. To instruct us in the life of true discipleship—John 8: 31.
    4. For imparting eternal life—John 8: 51.
    5. For laying unshakeable foundations of character—Matt. 7: 24, 25.

IV. Their Ultimate Place in Final Judgment. John 12: 48.

V. The Place We Should Accord Them in Our Lives.

"Let the Word of Christ dwell in you richly in all wisdom" (Col. 3: 16). This sentence in the translation of A. S. Way reads: "May the word Messiah speaks to you have in your hearts, in all its wealth, its home."

If the author might give the results of a personal study he made recently as an example of what new and fresh truths may come to one just from a simple consideration of the English text dealing with some one subject, he would like to look with the reader at a topic that he himself never thought of before as containing anything of particular interest or value. In 1 Corinthians 15: 52, we find the phrase: "for the trumpet shall sound"; and in 1 Thessalonians 4: 16, 17 we read: "For the Lord Himself shall descend from Heaven with a shout, with the voice of an archangel, and with *the trump* of God: and the dead in Christ shall rise first: then we which are alive and remain shall be caught up together with them in the clouds, to meet the Lord in the air: and so shall we ever be with the Lord." The first thing I did was to make a list of all the passages in the Bible in which the noun *trumpet* or the phrase *to blow with the trumpet* was found. This can be determined easily by the consulting of an English Concordance. Then I began to classify these passages. I found that the first blowing of a trumpet in the Bible is recorded in the nineteenth chapter of Exodus (vv. 13, 16, 19; see also 20: 18 and Heb. 12: 19). The teaching of this passage simply thrilled me. Notice that when the trumpet is blown, "the Lord came down" (v. 20). Furthermore, when the trumpet was blown, the people were to "come up to the Mount " (v. 13), " to meet with God " (v. 17). Furthermore, the Lord came down to the people " in a thick cloud " (vv. 9, 16). Finally, this was to be " on *the third day* in the morning " (v. 16). Now think of the blowing of the trumpet when our Lord returns for His Church—He will come down for us; He will come in the clouds of glory (Matt. 24: 30; 26: 64) ; we will be caught up to Him. And does not the phrase, " the third day " always speak ultimately of resurrection? Next, I carefully looked at what is called The Feast of Trumpets (Lev. 23: 23–25; Num. 29: 1–6). I found that here again the blowing of the trumpets was for the calling of " an holy convocation," *i. e.*, a gathering together of the Lord's people. Furthermore, I found that this feast of trumpets ushered in a Sabbath day, a time of rest, as our resurrection will begin for us a time of resting from our labors (notice especially 2 Thess. 1: 7 R. V.). Then I discovered in the tenth chapter of Numbers detailed instructions for the blowing of the silver trumpets " for the calling of the assembly, for the journeying of the camps " (v. 2). Here again you have the people of God coming together at the blowing of the trumpet, and you have them moving out from their temporary camp, starting on a journey for a new location, just as when the trumpet is blown on the day of our resurrection, we will abandon our earthly residence and our physical bodies, and will move out into our permanent home in glory, and take up a new life in resurrection bodies. How much fresh light these passages throw upon the blowing of the trumpet, which Paul twice tells us will occur when the dead in Christ are raised and when we are changed!

Finally, I asked myself the question, as I often have, what did Paul mean when he spoke of this as "the *last* trump"? And then I realized that, whenever the trumpets were blown in the Old Testament, they were not blown for Gentile, unbelieving people, or for the world as a whole, but for His own people. Thus, this blowing of the trumpet for which we wait is our last trumpet, *i.e.*, the last time God shall call us, because He calls us then into an eternal abiding in glory. It is true that in the Book of Revelation there is the blowing of the seven trumpets (chap. 8, 9), but these are for judgment. They have to do with the world under God's wrath, and have nothing to do with us as believers. Therefore the trumpet on the day of resurrection is the *last* one which you and I will hear for our personal response.

III. Further Suggestions About the Manner of Our Bible Study

1. *What Is the Best Time for Our Study of the Scriptures?* This is a most important question— the time when we ought to plan to devote ourselves regularly to a study of the Word of God. Above everything else it ought to be a time which we can have each day. The time for our Bible study should be as regular as the time for our meals and for our work. As a famous leader of college students said some years ago: "We ought to have a Medo-Persian hour—an unchangeable hour for our Bible study." It ought to be the time when our faculties are keenest. It is unfair to God, and unjust to our own souls, to

attempt the devotional study of the Scriptures late at night, when we are mentally and physically weary, and when we shall be greatly tempted to fall asleep before we get very far with our reading. It ought to be a time when we can have the greatest privacy and quiet, possibly before the rest of the family has arisen for the day, or when the children have gone to school. For most people this time will be in the morning. The impressions of the morning are the deepest. Beginning the day with the Word of God, we begin on a high level. We *begin* with strength for the day's work, and power against the day's temptations. Something we receive early in the morning, alone with God, we can use in passing on to others for their enrichment sometime during the hours of the day that ensue. If we do have our Bible study in the morning, then no matter what happens during the day, what unexpected engagements arise, nothing will then be able to shut out this sacred time which we so deeply need. John Ruskin said to the students of Oxford University, in urging them to read the Bible: " Make it the first daily business to understand some part of it clearly, and then the rest of the day to obey it in what you do understand." " My voice shalt Thou hear in the morning, O Lord; in the morning will I direct my prayer unto Thee, and will look up " (Psalm 5: 3; see also, Ex. 34: 2). The time for our devotional study may seem to be of secondary importance, but because the wrong time, or an indefinite time, or different times, are chosen by young Christians, many a plan for regular Bible study goes on the rocks. Let us get this hour settled in the programme of our lives, and then let nothing interfere with it. Keep it as an engagement with God, and hold it as sacred, and even more sacred, than an engagement with some high official or dearest friend.

2. *How Much of the Bible Shall I Read at One Time?* The question of how much of the Bible we shall read every day is one which will generally be determined by the method we are following in our study of the Bible, and by the time that we have at our disposal. If we are reading one chapter a day, then, of course, that at once determines how many verses will be read, sometimes more and sometimes less. A good rule, however, to follow, if the particular method we are using at any one time does not itself determine how much we shall read, is the one that George Müller followed in his own life. " I read," he once said, " until I come to a verse upon which I can lean my whole weight, and then stop." If a young person finds himself defeated in some struggle with sin, he will want to read until he comes to a passage which reveals some great promise of God for victory; and he will hold on to that one passage, even if it is but a line, possibly all week. If one is seeking guidance in a very difficult problem, he will want to read until some passage of Scripture clearly reveals the course he should take. Sometimes we shall find just the verse we want as soon as we open the Scriptures. At other times we may have to read for half an hour before any one passage in the Word of God really grips our hearts.

That we may receive some truth each morning in our Bible study is far more important than that we read so many verses or chapters. This was impressed

on me in my own devotional reading lately, when I
opened my Bible with the determination to read one
chapter in the book of Joshua each day. The first
day when I read as far as the fifth verse, I came on
the phrase, " I will not fail thee." I wondered just
what that verb *fail* might mean, and the concordance
told me it was the Hebrew word *raphah*, meaning " to
make feeble, let be feeble, desist." Then I discovered
that it was the very word used by Moses when he
assured the Israelites, just before his death, of God's
abiding faithfulness (Deut. 31: 6, 8). Years later it
was the word used by David, in encouraging his son
Solomon (1 Chron. 28: 20). Elsewhere it is translated
" forsake " (Deut. 4: 31; Ps. 138: 8). When I had
found out these precious promises of God's sustaining
grace I had enough for the day. The next day I went
back to the same chapter, and outlined its development
(which is given in a previous part of this book).

We should not, however, be stingy in the amount of
Scripture which we plan to read each day. Dr. Torrey
used to say that he made it a rule to read enough to
enable him to turn one page of the Bible every twenty-
four hours, but this was so mechanical with him, a rule
followed in his early days, that he said he actually had
to put a marker in the Bible to tell him where he left
off. It will probably astonish many to know that one
single, normal issue of the *Saturday Evening Post* contains as much reading matter as the entire New Testament. Thousands of people read the *Saturday Evening
Post* through every week. The number of Christians
who read the New Testament through every week, or
even one whole book of the New Testament every
week, are so few that we need not talk about it.

3. *The Art* The great devotional book of the Bible,
of Meditation the Psalms, opens, as we all know, with
the following words: " Blessed is the
man that walketh not in the counsel of the ungodly,
nor standeth in the way of sinners, nor sitteth in the
seat of the scornful. But his delight is in the law of
the Lord: and in His law doth he *meditate* day and
night " (Psalm 1: 1, 2). At the end of the nineteenth
Psalm, David prays: " Let the words of my mouth,
and the *meditation* of my heart, be acceptable in Thy
sight, O Lord, my Strength and my Redeemer." Again
and again the writer of the one hundred nineteenth
Psalm declares his determination to *meditate* in the
statutes of the Lord (vv. 15, 23, 48, 78, 97, 99, 148).
The Lord commanded Joshua, as he stood on the
threshold of his mighty work of conquest in Canaan:
" This book of the law shall not depart out of thy
mouth; but thou shalt *meditate* therein day and night,
that thou mayest observe to do according to all that
is written therein: for then thou shalt make thy way
prosperous, and then thou shalt have good success "
(Joshua 1: 8). Here is probably where many Christian people fail in their Bible study. They do not
know how really to feed upon the Word, to meditate
upon it, to incorporate it in their lives.

The late Dr. W. H. Griffith Thomas has said:
" ' Meditation ' comes from a Greek word meaning ' to
attend.' It is reading with *attention*. More than this,
it is reading with *intention*. It is concerned at each
point with personal application, and it must be our
thought, our own musing, our own application. Look
well at this text, made as clear as the printer's art can
emphasize its teaching: ' MY meditation of HIM '

(Psalm 104: 34). The great, the primary, the essential point is *first-hand* meditation on God's Word as the secret of Christian living. The hour of meditation is not a time for dreamy, vague imaginings, but for revealing actual blessing, whether in the form of guidance, comfort, or counsel." Andrew Murray, who found the richest things in the Word of God, and who was a master in the art of meditation, reminds us that: "It is in meditation that the heart holds and appropriates the Word. Just as in reflection the understanding grasps all the meaning of a truth, so in meditation the heart assimilates it and makes it a part of its own life. We need continual reminding that the heart means the will and the affection. The meditation of the heart implies desires, acceptance, surrender, love. What the heart truly believes, that it receives with love and joy, and allows to master and rule the life. The intellect gathers and prepares the food upon which we are to feed. In meditation the heart takes it in and feeds on it."

We should be careful not to give all of our time just to reading the Word, to see how much we can cover; but, after reading a portion, we should carefully, prayerfully turn it over in our minds, and appropriate it in our hearts. Some time ago a professor at the University of Wisconsin coined the word "retinize," which, he said, meant "to read with the eye," but not to understand with the mind. So much of our Bible reading is simply "retinizing" the written page without appropriating the living truth.

There is nothing finer on the need for meditation in our study of the Scriptures than the words which that mighty man of faith, George Müller, recorded in his diary, under the date of May 9, 1841, and I make no apologies for quoting it here, in spite of its length:

" It has pleased the Lord to teach me a truth, the benefit of which I have not lost for more than fourteen years. The point is this: I saw more clearly than ever that the first great primary business to which I ought to attend every day was, to have my soul happy in the Lord. The first thing to be concerned about was not how much I might serve the Lord, or how I might glorify the Lord; but how I might get my soul into a happy state, and how my inner man might be nourished. For I might seek to set the truth before the unconverted, I might seek to benefit believers, I might seek to relieve the distressed, I might in other ways seek to behave myself as it becomes a child of God in this world; and yet, not being happy in the Lord, and not being nourished and strengthened in my inner man day by day, all this might not be attended to in a right spirit. Before this time my practice had been, at least for ten years previously, as an habitual thing, to give myself to prayer after having dressed myself in the morning. Now, I saw that the most important thing I had to do was to give myself to the reading of the Word of God, and to meditation on it, that thus my heart might be comforted, encouraged, warned, reproved, instructed; and that thus, by means of the Word of God, whilst meditating on it, my heart might be brought into experimental communion with the Lord.

" I began therefore to meditate on the New Testament from the beginning early in the morning. The first thing I did, after having asked in a few words the Lord's blessing upon His precious Word, was to begin to meditate on the Word of God, searching as it were into every verse to get blessing out of it; not for the sake of the public ministry of the Word, not for the sake of preaching on what I had meditated upon, but for the sake of obtaining food for my own soul. The result I have found to be almost invariably this, that after a very few minutes my soul has been led to confession, or to thanksgiving, or to intercession, or to supplication; so that, though I did not, as it were, give myself to prayer, but to meditation, yet it turned almost immediately more or less into prayer. When thus I have been for a while making confession or intercession or supplication, or have given thanks, I go on to the next words or verse, turning all, as I go on, into prayer for myself or others, as the Word may lead to it, but still continually keeping before me that food for my own soul is the object of my meditation. The result of this is, that there is always a good deal of confession, thanksgiving, supplication, or intercession mingled with my meditation, and that my inner man almost invariably is ever sensibly nourished and strengthened, and that by breakfast time, with rare exceptions, I am in a peaceful if not happy state of heart. Thus also the Lord is pleased to communicate unto me that which, either very soon after or at a later time, I have found to become food for other believers, though it was not for the sake of the public ministry of the Word that I gave myself to meditation, but for the profit of my own inner man."

4. *The Value*   At the beginning of this study we
of Making Notes   said we wanted to be exceedingly
                            practical. We are now going to

suggest something that so few Bible teachers seem to find it necessary to recommend, and yet, after years of experience, we believe that it is one of the most essential aspects of personal, devotional Bible study. We refer to the making of notes. People can so easily read a page of the Bible and then give some time for meditating upon it, and actually think that they have profited by the half hour they have spent with the Word; but, if you were to ask them what they gleaned from the Word, that day, they would frequently find it difficult to put their fingers on any one rich truth that they had obtained. Another has well said: " The Bible study that is done in one's head is very apt to get out of one's head. Our heads aren't much. They don't hold very much. Our heads lose very fast what goes through them, and if we trust to retaining by our memories what we do in our Bible study, we shall lose most of it." If, however, each young Christian would have a little notebook and actually write down, morning by morning, what the Lord gives out of the verse he or she is meditating upon, it would be found that thoughts would be clarified, the profit derived from Bible study would be greatly increased, and a definite record of the things that the Holy Spirit has taught from day to day, and from week to week, would be had in permanent form. If one does not care to use a notebook, then let one use the margin of his Bible, providing it is a wide margin, and providing it will take ink. Never make permanent notes in pencil, because the very fact that one is writing his notes in pencil will make him feel that they are more or less of a temporary or superficial nature. The author knows of nothing that will so encourage careful reading of, and sincere meditation upon, the Word of God, delivering us from the great temptation to vagueness and indefiniteness, as a *recording* of what we have found from day to day, in our private note-book, or diary, or in the margins of our Bibles.

5. *The Holy Spirit Is Our Teacher*   When a young man in one of our city high schools today enters his junior year he usually finds in his schedule for study for that year the subject of chemistry. He probably knows absolutely nothing about it, not even its simplest truths, nor its most elementary formulas. But he is not handed a text-book on chemistry, with the instruction: " Master this subject." It is true he has a text-book. But he also has a *teacher,* and it is the task of that teacher to know what the book contains, and to guide that young man through the book so that he too will know what truths its pages contain. The Bible is a Book revealing spiritual truths, but, as Paul reminds us: " The natural man receiveth not the things of the Spirit of God: for they are foolishness unto him; and he cannot know them, because they are spiritually judged " (1 Cor. 2: 14 R. V.). A Christian, however, is not a *natural* man, but a *spiritual* man, for he has been born again of the Holy Spirit (John 3: 5, 6), and the Holy Spirit lives within him (Rom. 8: 9, 11, 16; Gal. 4: 6; etc.).

The Spirit of God is our Divine Teacher, for " the things of God none knoweth, save the Spirit of God. But we received, not the spirit of the world, but the Spirit which is from God; that we might know the things that are freely given to us of God " (1 Cor.

2: 11, 12 R.V.). Shortly before our Lord's death, He gave this profound promise: " Howbeit when He, the Spirit of Truth, is come, He shall guide you into all the truth: for He shall not speak from Himself; but what things soever He shall hear, these shall He speak: and He shall declare unto you the things that are to come. He shall glorify Me: for He shall take of Mine, and shall declare it unto you. All things whatsoever the Father hath are Mine: therefore said I, that He taketh of Mine, and shall declare it unto you " (John 16: 13–15 R. V. See also John 14: 17; 15: 26; 1 John 5: 6). The Swiss commentator, Godet, has well said: " The teaching by means of the Word can never give anything more than a confused idea of divine things; however skilfully this means may be used, it can only produce in the soul of the hearer an image of the truth. The teaching of the Spirit, on the contrary, causes the divine truth itself to enter into the soul; it gives it a full reality within us by making us have experience of it; it alone makes the Word a truth for us." As D. L. Moody once said: " The Bible without the Holy Spirit is a sun-dial by moonlight." The absolute need of the teaching of the Holy Spirit, especially in these last days, when there is so much *false* teaching, and such grievously erroneous interpretations of the Word, is clearly revealed in the First Epistle of John (see especially 2: 18–29).

It would be so helpful if the moment before opening our Bibles each morning we would ask the Holy Spirit to reveal to us the truth God has for us in the words we are about to read and meditate upon, remembering that He teaches those who are truly led by Him, and sanctified by Him.

6. *Praying into* There is no sweeter experience
Our Lives What than the daily habit of kneeling
God Gives to Us down at the desk, or table, or
in Our Bible Study chair where we have been studying the Word of God, and plead-
ing the promise we have found before the Throne of
Grace, or thanking God for some precious truth which
our hearts so greatly needed as the Word was opened
that morning. If the Word we have found rebukes
us, we should receive it with humility. If it reveals
a sin, we should ask God to deliver us from that sin.
If it shows us clearly what we should do that day,
whether to forgive another, to speak to some one about
the Lord Jesus Christ, to make a visit, to write a letter, to pay a bill, we ought at once to ask God for
strength and wisdom to do that which the Word has
commanded us. Probably a chapter will reveal anew
the glory and majesty of the Lord Jesus Christ, and
then we can but kneel down and adore Him, and
praise His wonderful Name.

7. *Bible Study* May the author of this book take
Means Study the liberty of warning all young
Christians about a very subtle form
of temptation they will have to meet on the very
threshold of beginning the study of the Bible? I refer
to the danger of forgetting that Bible study means
study, it means work, it will cost. Simply reading
your Bible does not mean you are getting spiritual
nourishment. Believing the Bible is not a synonym
for feeding on the Word. Bible study is the *study* of
the Bible, not dreaming over it, or arguing about it,
or defending it. Archbishop Trench has well said that

" Holy Scripture is not the Book for the slothful. It is a field, rather, upon the surface of which, if sometimes we gather manna easily and without labor, given as it were, freely to our hands, yet of which also many portions are to be cultivated with pains and toil, ere they will yield food for the use of man. This bread of life also is to be eaten in the wholesome sweat of our brows."

The Bereans *searched* the Scriptures (Acts 17: 11); Paul says that in dividing the Word of Truth we are to be *workmen* (2 Tim. 2: 15). Dr. G. Campbell Morgan, a mighty laborer in the Word, testifies after fifty years of Bible study: " The Bible yields its treasures to honest toil more readily than does any other serious literature. The Bible never yields to indolence." Do not put the blame for your failure in deriving real profit from the study of the Scriptures upon the Bible itself, or upon some person, if you have yourself failed to give it honest, consistent *study*.

8. *Never Be* Do not expect perfection in this great
Discouraged matter of the devotional study of the
Word of God. It is here that Satan will give you your hardest battle. When he first approached our parents, Adam and Eve, he threw doubt upon the Word of God, and then he denied that God had spoken. In the Parable of the Sower, we read that the great enemy of God, Satan himself, caught away the seed which was sown in the heart of the one who had heard the message of the kingdom. Probably every Christian has known the experience of resolutely determining never to let a day go by without the careful, prayerful reading of the Word of God, only

to know, after two or three weeks, of a day when, either through late rising, or an unexpected early morning call, or a crowded day, or through spiritual indifference, the Word was not read. *Do not let anything defeat you in this most important part of your Christian life.* It is the secret of everything! Defeat here is defeat all along the line! Even if you do lose a day, start again the next day. Even if something should come up and you should lose a whole week, or if your Bible should remain closed for a month, begin anew now, begin at once, determine the cause for your carelessness in this matter, the reason for ceasing such devotional study, and then ask God to deliver you from this temptation in the days to come. By all means, do not let Satan ever persuade you that this is a hopeless undertaking for you. Even if you have started and failed a dozen times, you can begin again *now*, with a greater longing than ever, with victory in that in which you formerly knew defeat.

9. *The Joyousness that Marks the Life of a Bible Student* There are many results in our lives that will inevitably accrue from a regular, devotional study of the Word of God, some of which we spoke about in the earlier part of this book, but, crowning them all, and because of the others—such as a greater knowledge of God, a cleansing from sin, victory in the hour of temptation, a new vision of service, a deeper peace in believing, a new vision of the glory of the Lord Jesus Christ—Bible study, whenever carried on sincerely, by the aid of the Holy Spirit, will result in abounding joy in the heart of the believer. This was the experience of the psalmist. " I

rejoice at Thy Word as one that findeth great spoil"
(119: 162. Cf. v. 14; 19: 8). This was the experience of the prophet Jeremiah: "Thy words were found
and I did eat them, and Thy Word was unto me the
joy and rejoicing of mine heart: for I am called by
Thy Name, O Lord God of hosts" (Jer. 15: 16). Our
Lord told His disciples that the words He gave to
them were spoken that His joy might remain in them
and that their joy might be full (John 15: 11). Those
same words continue to produce joy in the hearts of
all our Lord's disciples, down through every age. At
the beginning of the 24th chapter of Luke, we have
a picture of two disciples reasoning, debating, and
doubting in their hearts, mantled by a spirit of sad-
ness, as they walked together, bemoaning the death of
the Lord Jesus. The root of their sorrow and despair
was that they were "slow of heart to believe all that
the prophets have spoken" (v. 25). Later we find
their very hearts burning with a new joy, hope, and
confidence (v. 32). Why? Because the Lord, "beginning at Moses and all the prophets, expounded
unto them in all the Scriptures the things concerning Himself" (v. 27). The study of the Bible,
through which the Lord Jesus is beheld in the Word
of God, is the great cure for depression, for despond-
ency, for despair. The Ethiopian eunuch went on
his way rejoicing (Acts 8: 39), because the Word
of God had been opened to his heart, and, through
his reading and understanding of the Scriptures,
he had found the Lord Jesus as his Saviour.
Over every book of the Bible, and over the Bible as
one great Book, surely could be written the words
which the Apostle John wrote at the beginning of his

First Epistle: " These things write we unto you, that your joy might be full " (1 John 1: 4).

Years ago that peer of all preachers, Charles H. Spurgeon, wrote: " With what quiet joy does the plowman steal home with his golden find! How victors shout as they share the plunder! How glad should the man be who has discovered his portion in the promises of Holy Writ and is able to enjoy it for himself, knowing by the witness of the Holy Spirit that it is all his own! " After years and years of close, deep study of the Word of God, Dr. R. A. Torrey gave this splendid testimony: " Is there any joy purer than that which comes from properly directed study? But there is no other study that brings joy for a moment comparable to the joy that comes from proper Bible study. The joys that come from earnest study of various kinds—philosophical, scientific, historical, literary, and linguistic—have been among my chief joys for many years, nearly my whole life through, from early boyhood, but there has come into my heart, from Bible study, through digging into the gold mines of this wonderful and inexhaustible Book, a joy with which the joys that have come from all other forms of study are not worthy to be compared for one moment. There are no other joys like this."

IV. The Bible-Reading Habits of Four Well-Known Americans

In discussing the fascination of Biblical biographies in a previous part of this book, we quoted the late Professor Albert Cave as saying that, " lives of great men bring to our remembrance the possibilities of our own lives." What could be more helpful, more encouraging, now that we have surveyed the reasons *why* we should study the Bible, and many of the methods we might employ in actually undertaking such Bible study, than to discover the habits of Bible study in the lives of four outstanding citizens of our country, men of different occupations, and, more or less, of different periods of our national history? It is a comparatively simple matter to secure glowing eulogies of the Holy Scriptures from the writings and addresses of almost every great personage in our national life: whole books have been compiled giving these most interesting expressions of admiration for the Word of God. It is a far more difficult matter, however, to secure authentic records of how some of our great men *actually studied the Bible themselves,* definitely informing us about their regular habits of reading the Scriptures. It is only with the latter that this book will concern itself.

Yet, I saw very recently two remarkable statements concerning the pre-eminent value of the Word of God uttered by the two greatest souls that have ever adorned our nation's life, and, not recollecting myself ever having seen just these words before, the reader will pardon me if I step aside from the original purpose of this concluding section, to quote them. In one of his prayers, George Washington uttered a petition that might well be repeated every day, by every true child of God: " As Thou wouldst hear me calling upon Thee in my prayers, so give me grace to hear Thee calling on me in Thy Word. Grant that I may hear it with reverence, receive it with meekness, mingle it with faith and that it may accomplish in me, gracious God, the good work for which Thou hast sent it." Abraham Lincoln once said: " In regard to the great Book, I have only to say, it is the best gift which God has given men. All the good from the Saviour of the world is communicated to us through this Book."

The Sixth Presi- Every one reading this book knows
dent of the that the sixth President of the United
United States States was John Quincy Adams
                (1767–1848), but how many have
ever had the thrilling experience of reading the remarkable letters which he wrote to his son while he,
the father, was Minister of the United States to Russia? Perhaps before we look at the letters themselves,
those which have revealed the author's own personal
habits of Bible study, we might refresh our minds for
a moment in regard to Adams' personal history. With
little early schooling he accompanied his father to
France in 1778. After a short training in French and
Latin in an academy at Passy, he returned to America,
but went to France again in 1779 and attended the
Latin School at Amsterdam. He matriculated into
Leyden University in January, 1781, but soon went to
St. Petersburg as secretary to Francis Dana, United
States Minister to Russia. In 1783 he returned to
The Hague and resumed his classics under Dumas, the
Editor of Vattel. On the father's appointment to the
London mission the son determined to return to
America, entered Harvard College as a junior, grad-
uated in 1787, studied law at Newburyport under
Theophilus Parsons, afterwards chief justice of Massa-
chusetts, and was admitted to practice July 15, 1790.
Thus, by the age of twenty-three, Adams had an edu-

cation that could hardly be surpassed, and a rich experience in the capitals of Europe such as no young American of his day could boast of.

In 1809, when only thirty-two years of age, he was appointed by President Madison as United States Minister to Russia, and later, as Minister to the Court of St. James, in London. He was invited by President Monroe to become Secretary of State in his cabinet, in 1817, and in 1825 was elected the sixth President of the United States. Two years after the close of his term he was elected to the twenty-second Congress, and had the distinction of being returned for eight successive congresses, over a period of seventeen years. The verdict of such a man should carry as much weight as that of any man in public life in our country today. (A most interesting book would be one devoted to the religious convictions of all our Presidents.)

During his residence in St. Petersburg the future President of the United States wrote to his son, who was studying in a school in Massachusetts, a series of letters that have become famous. Those that have been published are devoted almost entirely to exhortations to read the Word of God. To give added effect to his earnest pleas, the father revealed some of his own habits of reading the Scriptures. "So great is my veneration for the Bible," he wrote, "and so strong my belief, that when duly read and meditated on, it is of all books in the world, that which contributes most to make men good, wise, and happy— that the earlier my children begin to read it, the more steadily they pursue the practice of reading it throughout their lives, the more lively and confident will be my hopes that they will prove useful citizens to their country, respectable members of society, and a real blessing to their parents.

" I advise you, my son, in whatever you read, and most of all in reading the Bible, to remember that it is for the purpose of making you wiser and more virtuous. I have myself, for many years, made it a practice to read through the Bible once every year. I have always endeavored to read it with the same spirit and temper of mind which I now recommend to you: that is, with the intention and desire that it may contribute to my advancement in wisdom and virtue. My custom is, to read four or five chapters every morning, immediately after rising from my bed. It employs about an hour of my time, and seems to me the most suitable manner of beginning the day. But, as other cares, duties, and occupations engage the remainder of it, I have perhaps never a sufficient portion of my time in meditation, upon what I have read. Every time I read the Book through, I understand some passages which I never understood before, and which I should have done, at a former reading, had it been effected with a sufficient degree of attention." It has been stated, upon good authority, that Mr. Adams continued these faithful daily habits of reading the Bible throughout his life, even during his crowded days while living in Washington.

He brings to a close this particular series of letters to his son with this final exhortation and prayer: " To read the Bible is of itself a laudable occupation and can scarcely fail of being a useful employment of time, but the habit of reflecting upon what you have read is equally essential as that of reading itself, to give it all the efficacy of which it is capable. I therefore recommend to you to set apart a small portion of every day to read one or more chapters of the Bible. . . . As an expedient for fixing your attention, make it also a practice for some time, to minute down in writing your reflections upon what you read from day to day; you may perhaps at first find this irksome, and your reflections scanty and unimportant, but they will soon become both easy and copious.

"And may the merciful Creator, Who gave the Scriptures for our instruction, bless your study of them, and make them to you ' fruitful of good works.' "

Emerson, who heard him in his later years, remarked: " No man could read the Bible with such powerful effect." It is of significance that Mr. Adams was a Vice President of the American Bible Society from 1818 to the time of his death, a period of thirty years.

America's Robert E. Lee is acknowledged by all mili-
Greatest tary students, both in this country and in
Soldier Europe, as one of the greatest soldiers of
the nineteenth century, and in many ways the greatest military strategist our own nation has ever produced. The integrity of his character, the absolute spotlessness of his own private life, can be surpassed by no famous figure in American history. Lee graduated from West Point in 1829, at the age of twenty-two, number two in his class, and without a demerit. He was made first lieutenant of engineers in 1836, and captain in 1838; at the age of forty-five he was appointed, against his wishes, superintendent at West Point. His achievements during the Civil War, toward the end of which he was general-in-chief of all

the Confederate armies, need not detain us here. After the War, as a recent writer on Lee has said, " His supreme interest was in restoring the economic, cultural, and political life of the South. His mail, which was immense, was crowded with offers of business proposals, all of which he rejected." In September, 1865, he accepted the presidency of Washington College, at Lexington, Virginia, which, after his death, October 12, 1870, changed its name in his honor to Washington and Lee University.

Lee's greatest biographer, Dr. Douglas S. Freeman, has summarized his influence and character as follows: " After sixty years, the affection and reverence of the South for him are, if anything, higher than in 1870. No American has ever had an influence on the people of the old Confederate states comparable to his. On all matters on which he expressed himself, he is still regarded as the final authority. In him, the South still sees the embodiment of all its best ideals. While Lee was distinguished as an educator, his place in American history is that of a notable Christian gentleman and a great soldier. He was confirmed in the Episcopal church in 1853, and the fundamentals of the Christian religion—humility, prayer, faith, and kindness—were his code of daily conduct. His equanimity was religious, rather than philosophical, and, though he was not a fatalist, he believed that God directed the affairs of man and ordered even man's adversities to his good. It was for this reason that he accepted defeat without repining. His unique relations with his soldiers, his affection for children, his dignified courtesy, and his love of animals are illustrated by a thousand anecdotes that are part of the spiritual treasury of Americans. His temper and patience seldom failed him. Self-control was second nature. His rare outbursts of wrath were generally followed by some particularly gracious act to the object of his displeasure."

What such a man thought of the Word of God, and what he did with the Word of God, will prove of the greatest interest. Dr. Freeman in his recently published monumental four-volume, *Life of Robert E. Lee,* further tells us that " The General had family prayers every morning, before breakfast, but his own spiritual life was bound up with the daily Bible reading and with special seasons of private devotions. The Bible was to him the Book of books, ' a Book,' he wrote, ' which supplies the place of all others, and which cannot be replaced by any other.' He received various copies of the Bible, both for himself and for the college, but the one he used was a pocket edition he had carried with him in all his campaigning since he had become a Lieutenant-Colonel in the United States army."

The Rev. J. William Jones, D.D., one of the chaplains of General Jackson, in an article written many years ago on " The Inner Life of Lee," tells us that " The Bible was his daily companion, his guide, his comfort, and his trust. He was a constant reader and a diligent student of God's Word, and had his regular seasons for this delightful exercise. In the army, he *read the Bible every day,* in his headquarters, on the march, in the bivouac; and he did everything in his power to circulate the Word of God among his soldiers." In a letter to Markie Williams, written in December after the close of the Civil War, Lee gave this splendid testimony: " I prefer the Bible to any other book. There is enough in that to satisfy the most ardent thirst for knowledge, to open the way to true wisdom; and to teach the only road to salvation and eternal happiness." Chaplain Jones records that Lee once said to him personally: " There are many things in the old Book which I may never be able to explain, but I accept it as the infallible Word of God, and receive its teachings as inspired by the Holy Ghost." And so, as Dr. Freeman finely says: " Simple as was his soul, he had ' meat to eat that ye know not of.' "

One of the Great Surgeons of the Twentieth Century In Gilman Hall, one of the beautiful buildings of Johns Hopkins University, Baltimore, there has hung for some years a famous painting of four great leaders in medicine and surgery whose brilliant work during the latter part of the nineteenth century and the early part of the present century made Johns Hopkins Hospital one of the great medical centres of the world. The four men who appear in this painting are Dr. William Osler, Dr. William Henry Welch, Dr. William S. Halstead, and the only one of the four still living, Dr. Howard A. Kelly. Dr. Kelly was Professor of Gynecology at Johns Hopkins University from 1889 to 1919, and Emeritus Professor and Consulting Gynecologist since 1919. For the last forty-four years he has been chief surgeon and radiologist in the famous Howard A. Kelly Hospital, Baltimore. The medical and surgical societies of which he is a fellow or an honorary member fill thirty lines in the much abbreviated sketch that appears in *Who's Who in America:* he has received honorary degrees from a number of institutions, including the University of Pennsylvania, and the University of Aberdeen, Scotland. Over twenty different volumes on gynecology, radiology, the appendix, medical biography, and other subjects, together with over five hundred scientific articles, have been written by this famous surgeon during the last half century. In this day, when science is so much admired, almost worshipped, and scientists are looked upon by so many as the one group of men worthy of our absolute confidence, surely the verdict of such a man demands our closest consideration, if it be concerning a subject to which he has given the full and unbiased attention of his vast mental powers. Dr. Kelly has devoted years and years of careful study to the Book this volume is discussing, and we will let Dr. Kelly tell us himself, first what he thinks of the Bible, and then, something of how he himself studies the Bible.

" I accept the Bible as the Word of God," Dr. Kelly says in his widely-known book, *A Scientific Man and the Bible,* " because of its own miraculous character, born in parts in the course of the ages and yet completed in one harmonious whole. Without the Bible, all God's precious parables in nature, His other book, are utterly lost, and nature, exploited merely for lucre or for the pride of science, is degraded and ruined. I testify that the Bible is the Word of God because it is food for the spirit just as definitely as bread and meat are food for the body. The Bible appeals to me strongly as a physician, because it is such excellent medicine; it has never yet failed to cure a single patient if only he took his prescription honestly. . . .

It is the one book in the world which reveals a God infinitely above our own natural imaginings, worthy of our love and worship, and inexhaustible in His wonderful nature. In opposition to false science and false religions it fixes the origin of sin at a particular time and in an individual, Satan, and at the very outset promises sin's cessation forever when that arch traitor shall be rendered forever impotent. It reveals God's righteousness in Christ, His judgment of sin, and His great mercy to every sinner who trusts Him. It is the one book in the world which is always young and fresh and inspiring. Whatever there is in civilization that is worth while rests on the Bible's precepts. Everywhere and in all its teachings the Bible claims to be the authoritative Word of God, and as such I accept it."

In a charmingly written booklet, which Dr. Kelly published some ten years ago, "How I Study My Bible," he said: "My conviction is that I must know His Word well; my Father has written me a letter and I must read it until I am acquainted with all its particulars. If I conceive of it as more than a mere letter and rather as a Will, a Covenant, I must then examine it searchingly as a lawyer scans a legal document, seeking to grasp its every shade of meaning to apply it to my life."

Every one who has ever heard Dr. Kelly speak about spiritual matters, who has ever seen him with his well-marked Bible open before him, and has had the privilege of hearing him tell of some of the rich things he has found in the Scriptures, will know what a real master of the Word this famous scientist is. It will be of the greatest profit to each one of us to have Dr.

Kelly tell us himself of his own habits of studying the Bible. In a personal letter to the writer of this book Dr. Kelly says: " I rise regularly at six in the morning and after dressing give all the time until our eight o'clock breakfast to the study of the Word. I find time for brief studies throughout the day and again in the evening. I make it a general rule to touch nothing but the Bible after the evening meal. It is the greatest possible help to me in my own spiritual life and growth, and enables me to carry fresh messages to my audiences. I have a feeling that the Bible is so profound a book that one ought to be able to give some fresh message to each and every audience year after year."

In the booklet which we referred to a moment ago he has given us further insight into his own habits of reading the Word. " One of my greatest helps in life," he writes, " is a red leather, hip-pocket notebook, opening lengthwise, of about a hundred pages, in which I jot down striking verses for meditation during the day, or record any succinct, well clarified, convincing statement touching the Bible or any spiritual truth. This serves to keep one on the *qui vive,* calling for constant, discriminating attention to what is read and heard, and serving to crystallize great thoughts in the memory and to foster the loftier habits of thinking."

Many people ask from time to time about the value of Bible helps, and the words of Dr. Kelly on this matter are worth quoting in this very place: " And how about the numerous Bible helps, the many good books written about the Bible? Invaluable and indispensable, but the help must always remain entirely subsidiary to the Word itself. Nothing is more futile than time spent reading religious and pious books, if the Bible is neglected, and yet many do that very thing because it seems easier."

But probably Dr. Kelly's most valuable paragraph on this great subject of the right method of Bible study is toward the very close of his discussion, and we take the liberty of copying it here in its entirety. " And now for my greatest secret for everyday common folks, known through the ages and yet ever needing to be restated and learned afresh as generation succeeds generation. It is this. The very best way to study the Bible is simply to read it daily with close attention and with prayer to see the light that shines from its pages, to meditate upon it, and to continue to read until somehow it works itself, its words, its expressions, its teachings, its habits of thought, and its presentation of God and His Christ into the very warp and woof of one's being. No, there is nothing remarkable about that, it is wonderfully simple. *But it works,* and one does come, in this way, to know the Bible and to understand it. What appears, to a beginner, as a great knowledge of the Bible is thus often only the natural result of a persevering use of the simplest of all methods, namely, reading the Book day by day until it becomes extremely familiar in all its parts."

In these days of great spiritual conflict, when we must avail ourselves of all the strength that God would place at our disposal for daily victory over sin, this final sentence from one like Dr. Kelly, whose life has been such a wonderful testimony to the redeeming and keeping power of God, comes with tremendous force to all of us who are earnestly and continually longing to be used by Him unto the uttermost. " Let my daily Bible then be my rock and my citadel, my high tower overlooking the city of Zion, where I dwell ~~secure from all the wiles of the enemy,~~ the sword of my spirit for defensive and offensive warfare on the arch enemy of our souls,—an armory full of weapons, not carnal, but spiritual and mighty through God to the casting down of strongholds."

An Outstanding   As a final testimony to the precious
Business Man   value of regular Bible study and the
                         place that men of large executive re-
sponsibilities have been able to give to it, the author of this book would like to use the name of a young business man of our own generation, Mr. Erling C. Olsen, the Executive Vice-President of The Fitch Investors' Service, Inc., of New York City. The Fitch Investors' Service publishes a complete line of financial and statistical services covering every branch of finance. These publications are used by banks, investment dealers, brokerage houses, and private and corporate investors. The Fitch organization also supervises over $500,000,000 of funds; that is, they advise and counsel on the investment of funds of banks, corporations, and other institutions, as well as the fortunes of private investors. The Fitch Investors' Service was organized in 1913, and Mr. Olsen has had complete charge of the concern since 1920. It is very interesting to know that the firm was showing a steady loss each year previous to 1920 when Mr. Olsen was asked to take charge of it, and he did so under the agreement made with his associate, Mr. John K. Fitch, that, if the Lord chose to prosper their work in the

future, they would give a certain portion of their annual earnings to definite Christian work, a covenant that has been faithfully kept ever since. Mr. Olsen is known to thousands of people throughout the East, especially around New York City and Philadelphia, as the one who broadcasts every Thursday evening and every Sunday morning over WMCA. His Sunday morning messages from the Psalms have had a tremendous circulation, as they have been printed in pamphlet form from week to week and year to year. These messages are worthy of taking their place along with the best contemporary studies of the Psalms published by any of our Christian scholars, even professors in theological seminaries and ordained ministers, though Mr. Olsen is distinctly a layman without theological training. The author of this book has asked Mr. Olsen to give us his personal testimony regarding his study of the Word of God, and it is our joy to pass this on to our readers for their own edification and encouragement.

"I came to know the Lord as my Saviour when I was 17 years of age. This decision took place in an Inquiry Room after a Sunday evening service while in company with a friend who also received Christ at the same time. Not a word was said between us as we later boarded the trolley to wend our way home until we approached the street where this friend was to leave. Then I suggested to him: 'I'll meet you at the prayer meeting on Wednesday night.' Of course, his response was in the affirmative—yet it did seem strange to talk about a prayer meeting when up to that time no one suggested the need of prayer meetings.

" When I arrived home I never said a word to any member of my family regarding the decision of the evening. I went to my room. The first thing I did was to read my Bible. The man who led us to Christ did not suggest that we should read our Bibles. In fact, not a word of instruction was given by him to us. I had read my Bible previously while attending Sunday school. I had studied it to memorize verses for Sunday school exercises yet, as far as I know, I had never turned to the Bible voluntarily, prior to that night. I was a little amazed. I did not understand why I instinctively turned to the ' Book,' but as I continued reading I began to understand why a born-again person goes to the Bible for his spiritual food.

" The next morning just as naturally as life I got on my knees and then read a portion of Scripture. The following Saturday night my friend and I met and related our experiences of the past week, as we had testified to the saving grace of Christ. Then we read together the eighth chapter of Romans. One thing stands out in my memory—we both commented on the eighteenth verse:

> ' For I reckon that the sufferings of
> this present time are not worthy to
> be compared with the glory which
> shall be revealed in us.'

As we had borne our testimony during the week, we were conscious of the lack of response on the part of our friends. We began to understand what it was to receive jibes from them for merely stating that we had come to know Christ as our Saviour and were deter-

mined to live for Him. My! What a comfort it was
to learn that the Bible declared ' the sufferings of this
present time are not worthy to be compared with the
glory that shall be revealed in us.' Of course, the suffering was not anything but it magnified itself in our
one week's experience. But here was the wonderful
promise of the glory to be revealed in us in the future!
That verse became a great incentive to further witness
for Christ. It was my first lesson from the Holy
Spirit, that the Bible contained the needed strength
for Christian living.

" From then on I read the Scriptures systematically
and with regularity. Occasionally a day has passed
when I have not taken my usual time both at morning
and at evening for private reading of the Word, but
they are very few in number. Later I observed a
distinction between private reading and studying.
Some of my early study was done with a group. While
too much cannot be said for the value of that type of
study, I soon found the need of private study of the
Word. I think I can safely say that, during the first
seven or eight years of my Christian life, I devoted
at least four nights a week to the study of the Word,
probably as much as four hours a night; and since
then, anywhere from three to ten hours a week—and
sometimes more. Sometimes it was hard work—but
the blessing was rich—so much so that at times I had
to close the Book, for it was all that I could take in.

" Then came opportunities for the ministry of His
Word. No one can have such opportunities without
feeling the urge to study and the need to be in the
presence of the Lord for wisdom, for strength and for
the needed message.

" I thoroughly believe that no study or training can take the place of systematic study and reading of the Bible, which not only equips one for appreciation of spiritual things, but is of incalculable value in properly weighing other things, such as the philosophies, the motives, and the thinking of men.

" The Bible has much to say about every phase of human life: our homes, our relationships one with the other, our manner of conducting business, and of course that means much in a business man's life. There was a time when I assumed that there was a distinction between secular work and so-called Christian work until the 'Word' impressed me with the fact that whatsoever we do we are to do it as unto the Lord. Thus one could typewrite unto the Lord, one could conduct his business unto the Lord—what an avenue that opened! That meant I had a right to bring our business problems before the Lord.

" I can honestly say that if I have enjoyed any measure of success in business it is due solely to the grace of God. My schooling was limited, but the Word of God sharpened my powers of discernment.

" One of the truly great opportunities for the ministry of God's Word has been the privilege given to me over the radio. I had prayed often that the Lord might open the way for me to give a series of consecutive Bible studies. I shall never forget the day that the radio broadcast was offered to me. At that time one of the popular songs of the world had a line in it, ' Did you ever see a dream walking? ' How the natural man evidenced itself in a spiritual mind, for I certainly ' saw a dream walking ' as the opportunity was presented and the realization of my hope and prayer had come.

" I believe the Holy Spirit guided when I chose the Book of the Psalms as an appropriate Book for a series of consecutive Bible Studies for Sunday mornings. It has been wonderfully interesting to observe the Lord's leading in the preparation of these messages and in their delivery. It would have been utterly impossible to have conducted this series were it not for the fact that much time had been spent in prior years in the study of the Scriptures. How little we know what the Lord has in store for us!

" I can honestly witness to the fact that the Lord Jesus and His Word, and the privileges of witnessing for Christ, are more precious to me now than they were when I first believed. As a young believer in my teens, I was disappointed to hear from older Christians that as one grew older the zeal of first love would wane; that one should not expect to have the same joy in the tenth year of the Christian life as he had during the first year. Such an experience is wholly unnecessary, and, in my judgment, is due entirely to failure to read the Scripture consistently and consecutively, meditating upon it and loving its ministry. The Bible is the *Written* Word, but it throbs with *Life.* It reveals the *Living Incarnate* Word—the Lord Jesus Christ. As the heart responds to the Person of Christ, so the heart and mind respond to the Word of Christ.

" I think my associates would bear with me in asserting that I devote every energy in a decidedly active business life. If there is one thing I trust I have accomplished, it has been to give the lie to the excuse that one is too busy for the study and meditation of the Word of God."

No remarks have been made in the preceding parts of this book regarding the testimony of President John Quincy Adams, General Robert E. Lee, and Dr. Howard A. Kelly, but the author can hardly refrain from pointing out one very important point in Mr. Olsen's testimony, and that is the way in which the Lord so wonderfully led him, in the early days of his Christian life, to give himself enthusiastically to a continuous study of the Word of God, and then how, after years of hard study, the Lord opened up wonderful opportunities for him to communicate to others the treasures which the Holy Spirit had given him from the Scriptures. Let it be said to any young person who may be reading this book that God may have for him a similar work; perhaps in a different part of our country, and perhaps along a somewhat different line, and yet a definite work of expounding and exalting the Word of God, if that young person will now give himself or herself to the reverent, faithful study of the Holy Scriptures. If the author of this book, who is a minister in the Presbyterian Church, may be allowed to make a personal statement here, he would say that it is his own conviction that true, clear, interesting, stimulating Biblical preaching, in which the Word of God is expounded in all of its fullness, is becoming increasingly rare in the pulpits of our country. (A statement that seems to be truer with each passing year.) Yet, on the other hand, it is the one thing supremely needed in these critical days for the strengthening of the hearts of those who are fainting, for the encouragement of those who are fearful, for the illumination of life's pathways in days that are growing increasingly dark and dangerous.

If there is to be in the days to come a great revival in our land, if we are to have a new era of powerful Gospel preaching, and clear Biblical teaching, it will only be because this generation of Christian young people will themselves solemnly vow before God to be faithful above everything else in their devotion to, and their study of the Word of God, and in living in the power of that Word for the glory of the Lord Jesus Christ, that God may mightily use them in the coming days " as lights in the world, holding forth the Word of life " (Phil. 2: 15, 16).

Forever, O Lord, Thy word is settled in Heaven.

Thy word is very pure: therefore Thy servant loveth it.

Open Thou mine eyes, that I may behold wondrous things out of Thy law.

I am Thy servant; give me understanding, that I may know Thy testimonies.

I will meditate in Thy precepts, and have respect unto Thy ways.

I will delight myself in Thy statutes: I will not forget Thy word.

I have refrained my feet from every evil way, that I might keep Thy word.

How sweet are Thy words unto my taste! Yea, sweeter than honey to my mouth.

Let my heart be sound in Thy statutes; that I be not ashamed.

Order my steps in Thy word: And let not any iniquity have dominion over me.

Mine eyes prevent the night watches, that I might meditate in Thy word.

Oh how love I Thy law! It is my meditation all the day.

Psalm 119: 89, 140, 18, 125, 15, 16, 101, 103, 80, 133, 148, 97.

V. Basic Books (and a Few Others) for the Bible Student's Library

By Way of   Of all the many and different ques-
Introduction   tions which have been asked of me by
               people writing from different parts of
the country, and by students coming into my office
from day to day, I think it can be said that half of
these questions have to do with the books which one,
as a Christian minister or student of the Bible, should
first read and (generally) purchase. The answering
of such questions, while a delightful task, is not, if
conscientiously done, an easy one. It is not only,
however, as an answer to the many questions which
frequently arise in the minds of many Bible students
concerning the best books which they ought to purchase that I have undertaken this bibliographical
study, but also that perhaps such a list might help
ministers and Bible students throughout our country
who are *not* asking such questions, but who ought to,
and who are confessedly improverishing their ministry
by not having in their study, and frequently using,
some of the great, stimulating works on biblical subjects. Over sixty years ago Bishop John Fletcher
Hurst, in the preface to his monumental *Literature of
Theology*, declared, with more succinctness and authority than any statement of mine on this point could
have, what in different places and in different ways I
have tried to express for some years past, and I take
the liberty here of quoting his excellent paragraph,
just as true today (possibly more so) as the day when
he wrote it: "That the average library of the Chris-

tian layman and of the minister of the Gospel is poor beyond words, is a lamentable fact. Many of the books are of such inferior authorship as to unfit them for even storage in any home of people either intelligent or hoping to be intelligent. Such books have drifted in because they are radiant with glaring and realistic pictures, or are bound in captivating sheep or calf, or are presented by well-meaning friends, or have been bought in lots at auction under the hallucination of cheapness, or because of some other apology for the existence of the trash. If two-thirds of the shelves of the typical domestic library were emptied of their burden, and choice books put in their stead, there would be reformation in intelligence and thought throughout the civilized world. A poor book is dear, and a good one cheap, at any cost. One's best book is that which treats best the suject on which one most needs light, and which one can get only by planning, by seeking, and often by sacrificing. One such book is worth more than all the diamonds of Golconda or the pearls of Tuticorin, and sweeter than all the perfumes of Araby the Blest. It is a friend for all seasons, and remains true to the eighties, and beyond, if they come. Better one shelf of such treasures than a shipload of literary driftings from the dead pyramids of publishers who sell slowly and of authors who fail quickly."

This volume, *Profitable Bible Study*, first appeared in 1939; the bibliographic part was somewhat revised for a second edition in 1950. This, then, is the third edition, and I have *completely rewritten* this part of the book. It has been a joy, for these something more than twenty years, to hear from ministers, teachers, missionaries, and lay-students of the Scriptures, of the help these pages have proved to them in the building of their own libraries. In fact, I am led to believe there are a great number of men engaged in Christian work today throughout the world who have built their library around this bibliography. From some I have had such enthusiastic statements as, "I have been able to get all but two of the books that you have mentioned."

How great the change has been in the evangelical publishing world since I first issued this list in 1939, particularly in two areas! In the first place, as soon as some hundreds of ministers and Bible students began asking for some of the books mentioned, which were out of print, some publishers began the reprinting of many of these volumes, until I would think that of the books mentioned that were then out of print, perhaps ninety percent of them are now available again. This is true, for example, of the great work on the Epistles of John, by Candlish; the four-volume *Christology of the Old Testament* by Hengstenberg, which Baker, of Grand Rapids, reprinted in 1952; the then very rare three-volume work by Peters on *The Theocratic Kingdom of Our Lord Jesus Christ,* for which I had the privilege of writing the Biographical Introduction; Alford's always valuable *Greek New Testament,* which my colleague, Dr. Harrison, has in part revised; *The Life of Our Lord Upon the Earth,* by Samuel J. Andrews, for which also I had the privilege of writing a biographical sketch when it was reprinted by Zondervan; etc.

The most marked difference, however, between a list of evangelical books written a quarter of a century ago, and one compiled today, is that we have so many more wonderfully rich, evangelical, authoritative volumes on almost every major aspect of Biblical interpretation, not available in 1939, and I hope I will be at least partially successful in now introducing my readers to some of these great works. In the two earlier editions, the title for this bibliographic material was "The First One Hundred Books for the Bible Student's Library," but the number is far over one hundred now, and hence, the change of the heading. I have tried here to set before the reader some of the most important books, in my own humble opinion, in most of the major departments of Biblical study. Another person compiling this list would, of course, omit some titles and add others.

Some Principles That Have Guided the Author in the Choice of the Volumes Suggested The basic principles which I have allowed to guide me in the choice of the works referred to should be explained. To begin with, it is absolutely impossible for any one man to know all the good books, even all the major books, that have been written around the Word of God, and the person and work of our Lord Jesus Christ.[1] Moreover, capacities for reading and study are so different among people: a high school student of ordinary intelligence can read one type of books relating to the Bible with pleasure and profit, but would be utterly lost in a commentary on the Greek text of Mark's Gospel, even though such a commentary might be acknowledged to be one of the most important books on this part of the New Testament written in the last fifty years. On the other hand, a graduate of a theological seminary, with a thorough training in Greek, might find a book recommended to the high school student quite elementary and unprofitable, while his mind and heart would be thrilled with the rich things brought forth from the Greek text of such a commentary on Mark's Gospel as Swete's. Again, a man or woman employed all day in business, or laboring on a farm, with perhaps only eight hours a week for Bible study (generally in preparation for a Sunday school lesson), must have literature suggested to him or her which can be read without too much effort, which can be more or less readily digested, and which must contain stimulating paragraphs, suggestive expositions, and practical interpretations. A person, however, who is giving his entire life to the Christian ministry, with five or six hours each day for study, would need to have volumes quite different from the books we would suggest to the other. Frankly, there is not known to the author of this article any *one* single book which *must* be suggested to *any one* who asks the broad sweeping question, "What one book shall I purchase to help me to understand the Word of God?" Depend upon it, a real knowledge of the Word of God will never come by the reading of any one book.

There are in this country today some 3,000 men and women who are teachers in theological seminaries and teachers of Bible and biblical subjects in the principal colleges of our land. There are approximately one hundred thousand men actively engaged as pastors in the Protestant denominations of our country. In addition to all these, there are estimated to be approximately two million two hundred thousand teachers and officers in the Sunday schools of Protestant churches in our country; how many of these are teachers, as distinguished from officers, there seems to be no way of ascertaining. Now I suppose there will be some professors of theology, and even professors of biblical literature in our colleges and seminaries, who will be severely critical of the one who has compiled this list, because he has included some works that are not written distinctly for advanced scholars, but can be understood by an ordinary layman who is determined to apply himself to study. Well, during an active pastorate of some twenty years, knowing the necessity of preparing from three to five new messages each week, for at least forty-five weeks of the year, in addition to many messages each year for Bible conferences, I have, in this list, had in mind the busy pastor, the Sunday school teacher, the Bible conference speaker, and those thousands of people who must continually stand up before the public and present some of the glorious themes and inexhaustible treasures of the Word of God. For this reason, then, e.g., I have not even mentioned such a volume as the one on Genesis in the *International Critical Commentary*, which, I suppose, is a very good work on the Hebrew vocabulary of the text of Genesis, but every time I have turned to it, I have come away feeling that a dry Sahara wind has swept across my soul. If this list were made for a few thousand expert scholars in biblical subjects, it would be an altogether different list, but I feel that experts in biblical subjects do not need such a list; they can make their own, and generally do not care for suggestions of this kind from other people, nor do I blame them. I am compiling this list, not for a few thousand of the most advanced Bible scholars in America, but for that group of one hundred thousand men and women who are really seeking help in their ~~study of the Word of God~~, and through whose lips and writings most of what evangelicals believe about the Word of God is enunciated and defined.

Still, recognizing these differences, I have tried to draw up a list of books which will be helpful to *every one* who is in any way seriously interested in Bible study. I do not mean all these books will be of value to all people, but that all people interested in Bible study will find some books here of pre-eminent value.

In attempting to help students in the study of the Bible, I have felt that one should seek to encourage more than a mere intellectual grasp of the contents of Holy Scripture. Students of other literatures may become masters of their subject by the constant application of their intellect alone—but the Word of God is for *all* of man's nature, and a study of it should result in a love for the Word, obedience to the Word, holiness of life, growth in grace, in a knowledge of our Lord and Saviour Jesus Christ, a passion for communicating the truths discovered to others (2 Timothy 2:2), and a full, rich equipment for effective Christian service. "All Scripture is inspired by God, and may profitably be used for teaching, for confutation, for correction, and for righteous discipline; that the man of God may be fully prepared, and thoroughly furnished for every good work." (Translation of W. J. Conybeare.) Thus I have not hesitated, at times, to include works especially valuable for their inspirational pages, books that lead us to the throne of grace, that compel us to pray, and that make us not only better scholars, but better *men of God*.

In constructing such a list of books, may I frankly confess, that I do not think anyone giving himself to a lifetime of Bible study should acquire, first of all, every book in this list, before he begins to acquire other volumes relating to Biblical interpretation not referred to here. Every minister will, if he is enthusiastically interested in the Scriptures, have some special field or fields in which he is more deeply interested, and in which he will be reading as widely as time and circumstances will allow. Furthermore, many ministers will wisely undertake, from time to time, series of sermons on some particular book of the Bible, or some Biblical character, or a great doctrine of the Christian faith. If, e.g., he is preaching an extended series of sermons on St. Paul's Epistle to the Ephesians, he will want to gather together at once, as far as his means will permit, the principal commentaries on this Epistle, before some of the other books in this list are purchased. It is inevitable that some will wonder why certain volumes that have proved a great blessing to them personally are not here listed. But may I emphasize the fact that such a list as this can, if it is honestly done, only be the result of the writer's personal acquaintance with Biblical literature, and I must confess I am not able to read, or even examine, year by year, all the hundreds of books that are appearing relating to the inexhaustible themes of the Holy Scriptures, not even all the important ones.

As far as possible, the latest edition of any particular work is given. As a rule, I have not allowed myself to be guided by the matter of price, though in a number of cases, I have included in parenthesis references to less expensive volumes in certain areas, such as Bible Atlases etc. Though it is not good bibliographic procedure, when the pagination of a volume is broken and different parts of the book have separate page sequences, I have sometimes taken the liberty of giving the total number of pages rather than separate figures. Thus, in Young's *Analytical Concordance*, the pages actually are 1090, 93, 23, and 45, and I have simply given the total as 1251.

BIBLES

The question of what version of the Bibles to use in reading and studying, is now not only a most important matter, but is bringing increasing confusion, I am afraid, to the Christian church. There are available today more versions of the Scriptures than any one person can master, and I, for one, would not dogmatically say that consulting ten or twelve different English versions in the study of a given text, necessarily leads to a sound knowledge of the Scriptures. All the modern versions have some commendable qualities, and also have weaknesses, and sometimes very regrettable features. I still think that the best discussion is found in the older work by H. S. Miller: *General Biblical Introduction*, Houghton, New York, 1937. A brief list of works surveying these modern editions will be found later in these pages.

In addition to the great indispensable King James' Version, I would still recommend the American Revised Version published in 1901, and then, of course, the new widely used Revised Standard Version, also published by Nelson, the New Testament in 1946, and the complete Bible in 1960. (Ten million copies have been sold in the last nine years.) Incidentally, there has recently been published a remarkable volume on the men who made the King James' Version, entitled *The Learned Men* by G. S. Paine (New York, Crowell, 1959). Among the most important of the other versions, I would certainly recommend the brilliant work by J. B. Phillips: *The New Testament in Modern English,* Macmillan, 1959, and especially the translation of the Book of Acts, *The Young Church in Action,* originally published in 1955. On an unforgettable day in 1950, there walked into my office, one who immediately took his place in the inner circle of my heart, the well-known author, Norman P. Grubb, who during the afternoon asked me if I had a copy of *The New Testament in the Revised Version of 1881 with Fuller References,* published by the Cambridge University Press in 1910. I not only did not have the book, I had never heard of it, though this embarrassment was not as acute as it might have been, when I discovered that no other member of my faculty had ever heard of it either. This is simply the New Testament with an elaborate apparatus of Biblical references, produced after years of work, by Albert William Greenup and the famous Greek scholar, James Hope Moulton. It is a library in itself, and it is strange how few have ever heard of it. When it came into my possession, I wrote to the publishers and was able to secure the last six copies that they had for my friends. One will find it very difficult to pick up second-hand. Without explaining here the meaning of the various marks used in the reference system, I would like simply to give an illustration of what has been done with one sentence, Matthew 1: 22, 23.

~~Now all this is come to pass,~~ [d]that it might be fulfilled which was spoken by the Lord [f]through the prophet, saying,

23[g]Behold, the [h]virgin shall be with child, and shall bring forth a son,

And they shall call his name [6i]Immanuel;

which is, being interpreted, God[j] with us.

22[d]ch. 21: 4, 26: 56; cp. Jn. 19: 36. [e]ch. 2: 15, 23, 4: 14, 8: 17, 12: 17, 13: 35, 21: 4, 26: 56, Mk. 14: 49; cp. ch. 2: 17, 13: 14, 26: 54, 27: 9, Jn. 2: 22, Ja. 2: 23; see Lk. 21: 22 and Jn. 13: 18. [f]ch. 2: 5, 15, 17, 3: 3, 4: 14, 8: 17, 12: 17, 13: 35, 21: 4, 24: 15, 27: 9, Ac. 2: 16, 28: 25; cp. ch. 2: 23, 26: 56, Lk. 1: 70, 18: 31, 24: 25, 44, Jn. 1: 45, 6: 45, Ac. 3: 18, 21, 7: 42, Ro. 1: 2, al.

23[g]Cited from Is. 7: 14; cp. Is. 9: 6. [h]Gn. 24: 43 (Heb.), Ex. 2: 8 (Heb.), Ps. 68: 25 (Heb.), Pr. 30: 19 (Heb.). [i]Is. 8: 8, 10. [j]See ch. 28: 20.

6[6]Gr. *Emmanuel.*

Thousands of Bible students have been taught and strengthened by the material presented to them in the *Scofield Reference Bible,* originally published, with the cooperation of seven editors, by the Oxford University Press in 1909, with a revision in 1917. Having had the priviledge of being a member of the Committee which met for five years in constructing a complete revision of the Scofield Bible, to be published in 1964, I would like to give it as my own verdict that this will be, I think, recognized everywhere as the most helpful reference Bible yet to be published in the English language.

For those who are interested in the Biblical text,

both in the original languages and in Latin, French, and German, as well as English, there is nothing, of course, to compare with the *Hexaglot Bible*, the subtitle of which indicates its contents: *Comprising the Holy Scriptures of the Old and New Testaments in the Original Texts together with the Septuagint, the Syriac (of the New Testament), the Vulgate, the Authorized English, and German, and the Most Approved French Versions; Arranged in Parallel Columns.* The editing of this work was done by Dr. Edward Riches de Levante, assisted by a number of biblical scholars, and was originally published in this country by Funk & Wagnalls, in 1909. The work is in six quarto volumes (12x9½ inches), with a total number of 4354 pages. One may not need to consult this work often, yet when one wants to see how a certain verse reads in the Septuagint, in the Latin Vulgate text, or in a German or French version, he can instantly find what he wants in these volumes.

For those who are interested in the earlier English versions, there has just been published by Thomas Nelson and Sons, a large quarto of 1500 double column pages, entitled *The New Testament Octapla*, edited by Dr. Luther A. Weigle of the Yale Divinity School. Here one has in parallel paragraphs the full text for the New Testament of the translations of Tyndale, 1525; the Great Bible, 1539; the Geneva Bible, 1560; the Bishop's Bible, 1568, the Rheims Bible, 1582; the King James text of 1611; the Revised Version of 1881 (or the American Standard Version of 1901); and finally, the Revised Standard Version of 1946. Dr. Weigle has written an introduction on the early English translations of the Bible, and there are full page photographs of the title pages of all these eight versions—a basic work for any careful study in the history of our English versions.

CONCORDANCES

In regard to concordances, an indispensable tool for any Bible student, some will disagree. Personally, I have always held that the best concordance to the King James version is the *Analytical Concordance to the Bible* by Robert Young, first appearing in 1880.[2] The latest edition (20th ed., 1938) carries an authoritative and invaluable supplement, "Recent Discoveries in Bible Lands," by Dr. William F. Albright, for many years the director of the American School of Oriental Research in Jerusalem, and until his recent retirement, the W. W. Spence professor of Semitic Languages at Johns Hopkins University. It is almost wicked to repeat the "clever," but iniquitous and distinctly false verdict, "Cruden's for the crude, Young's for the young, and Strong's for the strong." It is estimated that Young's work contains 311,000 separate references to words and phrases in the Old and New Testaments (118,000 more than in any other concordance).[2]

The Complete Concordance to the American Standard Version of the Holy Bible in the Revised Edition, by M. C. Hazard (New York, 1922) gives no material concerning Hebrew and Greek words, but alphabetically divides the references to most words into groups, arranging them under phrases in which one word is prominent. Thus, the one word "house" has three columns of references, and then all the references to the phrase, "house of Ahab" are given, then all the references in which the phrase "all the house" appears, then all the references having such phrases as "house of Baal," "house of bondage," "breeches of the house," "build *with* house," "house *with* father," "her father's house," "his father's house," "my father's house," "our father's house," "thy father's house," "father's house," "house of God," "her house," "his house," "his own house," "in the house," etc, etc. Forty-five divisions are given under this one word *house*.

BIBLE DICTIONARIES

In the very month I am working at the revision of this bibliographic material, there has been issued what is indisputably the most important one-volume Bible Dictionary to appear in our language during the last sixty years. I refer to *The New Bible Dictionary*, the result of some years of work by the Inter-Varsity Christian Fellowship of London. It contains hundreds of articles of the highest scholarship, evangelical throughout, the product of the work of some 140 contributors, including epochal articles by Professor F. F. Bruce and Professor Donald J. Wiseman. This truly great work is enriched by extensive bibliographies, gives us the latest data regarding all archaeological research in Biblical lands, and superb articles on most of the great doctrines of the Christian faith etc, etc. The volume contains approximately 1,600,000 words of text, and must be considered from now on as an indispensable tool for all seriously-minded Bible students.

The great *International Standard Bible Encyclopedia*, thoroughly revised in 1930, and now published by Eerdmans, in five quarto volumes, is undergoing complete revision again, under the editorial supervision, with a large staff of contributors, by Dr. Everett F. Harrison and Dr. Geoffrey Bromiley of Fuller Theological Seminary. *Davis Dictionary of the Bible* still has value, particularly the last edition which Dr. Davis himself did.

The much older work, by Dr. William Smith, with the simple title, *Dictionary of the Bible,* is still of real value, especially the American edition, revised and edited by H. B. Hackett and Ezra Abbot, in four handsome volumes, New York, 1871. Smith's *Dictionary of the Bible* went through numerous editions, abridgments, etc. and its articles on such matters as Biblical Flora, Biblical Geology, etc. have never been equaled in any other Bible dictionary.

Of all the famous Bible Dictionaries edited by the late James Hastings, I have found the most valuable one to be the two-volume work, *A Dictionary of Christ and the Gospels,* New York, 1906–1908. In these volumes are some really magnificent discussions of many of the subjects which are continually occupying a minister's thought, articles to which he will have occasion to constantly turn, some of them being simply superb, and most of them exceedingly interesting and suggestive, e.g., the article "Boyhood of Jesus," by George Farmer (11 columns), "The Christian Calendar," by Maclean (15 columns); and that epochal study of the "Character of Christ," by Kilpatrick (35 columns). To one's surprise, Dr. Warfield writes the article "Children" (7 columns), and a great one it is. James Denney writes the article "The Holy Spirit" (25 columns). One could not ask for a better study of Nathaniel than the one here written by Alfred Plummer. The article, "Preaching Christ" by James

Denney (21 columns), will stir the soul of any minister; and, better than many books on the subject, is James Orr's massive treatment of the subject, "Redemption" (21 columns).   At the end of the *Dictionary of Christ and the Gospels* are articles on "Christ and the Early Church," "Christ in the Early Ages," "Christ in Reformed Thought," "Christ in Modern Thought," "Christ in Jewish Literature," "Christ in Modern Literature."   In the two volume *Dictionary of the Apostolic Church*, there are elaborate articles on all the principal cities which were touched by the Apostle Paul, on all the main characters, men and women, who appear in the book of Acts, and the New Testament Epistles, good introductory studies to the New Testament books, and special articles on such subjects as "Hellenistic and Biblical Greek" (17 columns), a long article on the difficult subject, "Sibylline Oracles," (28 columns), and, if one cares for the subject, a interminable article by Dr. James Moffatt on "War" (54 columns).   To read one article each day in one of these volumes would be to wonderfully enrich one's mind.

A number of other Bible Dictionaries will soon be appearing, one to be published by Zondervan, edited by Dr. Merrill Tenney of the Graduate School of Wheaton College, and another to be published by Moody Press, edited by Dr. Charles F. Pfeiffer, of the Gordon School of Theology and Missions.[3]

THE BIBLE: INTRODUCTORY WORKS

The number of books which attempt to give a general introduction to the Scriptures, with one emphasis or another, are legion, and only a few can be mentioned here. First of all, may I say that because of the restrictions of this bibliography, I will not include titles bearing upon the subjects of Canonicity, and the Hebrew and Greek texts. Excellent articles, and full bibliographies, on these subjects, and many others, may be found in the superb articles of *The New Bible Dictionary*. For the serious student, I strongly commend the careful reading of the volume by F. F. Bruce, *The Books and the Parchments* (Revell, 1950), which begins with a chapter on Books and Parchments, followed by chapters on the Alphabet, The Hebrew, Aramaic, and Greek Languages, The Canon of Scripture, the Text of the Old Testament, the Septuagint, the Text of the New Testament, the Latin Bible, the English Bible, etc., concluding with an excellent bibliography.

Most of a minister's study will be, in large part, within the New Testament, and so I am only mentioning Lexicons of this part of the Bible. There are really only four that one needs to consider. The older one is by Joseph Henry Thayer, *A Greek English Lexicon of the New Testament* (corrected edition 1889), a quarto volume. Personally, when I find that a minister who has attended seminary, and therefore has been taught Greek, does not have a Thayer's *Lexicon* in his library, I know at once that he is not a serious student of the New Testament Scriptures, and a man who is not should hesitate a long time before thinking that he has a right to stand up in the pulpit and open the Word of God to waiting souls. By this I do not at all mean that a man must know Greek before he can preach. The great work by James Hope Moulton and George Milligan, *The Vocabulary of the Greek*

Testament, Illustrated from the Papyri and Other Nonliterary Sources (London, 1930) is, of course, a storehouse of rich materials, but it does not give the definitions of words found in Thayer, it does not list all the Greek words used in the New Testament, and its price places it out of reach of most ministers (it is listed at $30). It is not a substitute for Thayer, but a supplement to it. A work of vast learning, by one of the greatest Greek scholars of the world in his day, far more theological than Thayer's work, though not listing all the words found in the Greek New Testament, is the *Biblico-Theological Lexicon of New Testament Greek*, by Hermann Cremer (4th edition, Edinburgh, 1895, T. & T. Clark). This volume is in many ways the equivalent of a whole library of theological and philological works. By far the most important Lexicon to be published in English since Thayer is an English translation of the epochal work of Walter Bauer, with corrections, etc. by William F. Arndt and F. William Gingrich, published by the University of Chicago in 1957, *A Greek English Lexicon of the New Testament and Other Early Christian Literature*. This will be an indispensable tool for New Testament students for many years to come. Among the rich features of this work are the hundreds of bibliographies, appended to the discussions of the Greek words. But it is not perfect. Recently in turning to the very important word in II Timothy 3: 16, *theopneustia*, translated "inspired of God," I was amazed to find only four lines of text, with no reference to literature. How could they have overlooked the magnificent treatment of this verse in B. B. Warfield's *Revelation and Inspiration* (pp. 229–280)?

I certainly want enthusiastically and earnestly to recommend to all New Testament students, the *Englishman's Greek Concordance of the New Testament* (9th edition, London, Bagster, 1908). This contains an arrangement of all the Greek words in the New Testament, arranged in alphabetical order, with a complete list of all the occurrences of each separate word, in their canonical order, with a full line for each verse in which that word occurs. Thus, for example, under *pneuma* you have the complete list of its nearly 400 occurrences, and can tell instantly whether the verse refers to man's spirit, the Spirit of God, the spirit of the age, etc. In an appendix is a list of all the English words in the New Testament Revised Version, with the various Greek words thus translated. For example, under *ordain,* there are ten different Greek words, and the pages where these may be found in the Concordance are indicated. I would never be without this work.

VERSIONS

As I have previously said, there are so many English versions now on the market that Christians are bound to become confused. All I would do here is to recommend three volumes that will prove an excellent guide to this accumulated mass of material. Dr. Henry Wheeler Robinson edited a standard work in 1954, *The Bible in Its Ancient and English Versions* (Oxford). A later volume is E. H. Robertson's *The New Translations of the Bible* (Naperville, Illinois, Allenson, 1959), which has the great virtue of full discussions of the various translations of specific passages, especially in the New Testament. Finally, and possibly the best of all (how he produces all these scholarly works, nobody knows), is *The English Bible, a History of Translations,* by Professor F. F. Bruce (Oxford, 1961). Don't forget that the older work by Bishop B. F. Westcott is still of great value, *A General View of the History of the English Bible* (3rd edition, rev., Macmillan, 1905).

INSPIRATION

The subject of the inspiration of the Scriptures is probably the most basically important one confronting the Christian Church at this time. Evangelicalism is fortunate in having some worthwhile literature on this theme. The best of the more recent studies is the work edited by Dr. Carl F. H. Henry, *Revelation and the Bible* (Grand Rapids: Baker Book House, 1959), a series of twenty-four studies by outstanding British, Continental and American scholars, on General Revelation, Special Revelation, Contemporary Views of Revelation, Christ's Use of the Scriptures, the New Testament Use of the Old Testament, the Canon, Contemporary Ideas of Inspiration, the Holy Spirit and the Scriptures, Archaeological Confirmations, Reversals of Old Testament and New Testament Criticism, etc. No work on these subjects of such significance has been issued in the English language since the great studies of Warfield of a half-century ago. Other worthwhile works are: Edward J. Young: *Thy Word is Truth: Some Thoughts on the Biblical Doctrine of Inspiration* (Grand Rapids, Eerdmans, 1957) one of the finest books on this subject, from a conservative viewpoint, published in recent years, frankly facing the major problems. An excellent volume is John F. Walvoord (ed.): *Inspiration and Interpretation*

(Grand Rapids, Eerdmans, 1957), a series of twelve studies by men who have specialized in the subjects treated, e.g., the Biblical Interpretation of Irenaeus; Luther and the Bible; Calvin and the Holy Scriptures; John Wesley as an Interpreter of Scripture; H. H. Rowley and the New Trend in Biblical Studies; Emil Brunner's Doctrine of Scripture; Reinhold Niebuhr's View of Scripture, and the concluding chapter by Dr. Carl F. H. Henry on Divine Revelation and the Bible.

A work that has not received the attention it deserves, outside of Lutheran circles, is Theodore Engelder's *Scripture Cannot Be Broken* (St. Louis, Concordia, 1945). Here is an excellent chapter on "Has the Bible Moral Blemishes?". Four chapters, embracing some 150 pages, are devoted to a vigorous defense of the doctrine of Verbal Inspiration. An earlier volume, still worth reading, is *The Philosophy of Revelation* by the late Dr. Herman Bavinck (London, 1909), one of the most famous of all the Stone Lectures delivered at Princeton Theological Seminary.

BIBLICAL INTERPRETATION: HERMENEUTICS

In the important field of Biblical Interpretation what we need today is a large comprehensive work, thoroughly conservative, on the scale of *the Biblical Hermeneutics* by Milton S. Terry, first published in 1883. Until that book is produced, we are glad to have the excellent volume by Dr. Bernard Ramm, *Protestant Biblical Interpretation, a Textbook of Hermeneutics for Conservative Protestants* (Natick, Mass.: W. A. Wilde Co., rev. ed., 1957).

Inasmuch as the history of Biblical interpretation is

one of the utmost importance, one will want to read James D. Wood: *The Interpretation of the Bible, An Historical Introduction* (London: Gerald Duckworth and Co., 1958). This is an able work, down to the chapter on the nineteenth century, where the conservative scholars of that era are not given the consideration they deserve. In his introduction, the author rightly says that with all the best aids of modern scholarship, "the modern interpreter requires, as did his predecessors, all the gifts and graces which come to him through the Holy Spirit." He concludes: "The work of interpretation requires to be done today, because through it men are brought face to face with Him Who is the Lord of Scripture."

BIBLICAL ARCHAEOLOGY

There is an enormous amount of material today, and much of it very important, relating to the various facets of the exciting subject of Biblical archaeology. The work that is generally stated to be the standard volume is the *Biblical Archaeology* of Professor George E. Wright of Harvard (Philadelphia, Westminster Press, 1957. An abridged edition, paper-back, is available at a much lower price).

A smaller work is by Donald J. Wiseman, formerly of the British Museum, now Professor of Assyriology at the University of London, *Illustrations from Biblical Archaeology* (Eerdmans, Grand Rapids, 1958). In my opinion the best conservative introductory work, with adequate bibliography, for the Old Testament data, is *Archaeology of the Old Testament* by Merrill F. Unger (Grand Rapids, Zondervan, 1954), and I am happy to say that the same publishers will be bringing out this year Professor Unger's newer work, *Archeology of the New Testament*. Of course, the greatest authority in Biblical archaeology in the world today is William F. Albright. Of his works, one might begin with the epochal *From the Stone Age to Christianity* (Baltimore, John Hopkins Press, 1940), also now appearing as a paper-back. Then one needs to have his *Archeology of Palestine* (revised ed., 1954; also in paper-back, in the Penguin series), and, finally, his *Recent Discoveries in Bible Lands* (Pittsburgh, Biblical Colloquium, 1956). If one can afford it, and is interested in such a subject, he certainly should secure the widely acclaimed volume edited by James B. Pritchard, *Ancient Near Eastern Texts Relating to the Old Testament* (2nd ed., Princeton, 1955), which was followed by the same editor's work, *The Ancient Near East in Pictures Relating to the Old Testament* (Princeton, 1954).

I hardly know what to recommend for the Dead Sea Scrolls. An indication of the extent of the literature is the work by my colleague, William Sanford LaSor, *Bibliography of the Dead Sea Scrolls, 1948–1957,* in which are listed more than 2300 different items pertaining to this subject, embracing the writings of some 700 different authors in nine languages! The list of periodicals alone has 179 entries. This was published in the *Fuller Library Bulletin*, Fall, 1958. Let me mention only four books here. Millar Burrows: *The Dead Sea Scrolls* (New York, Viking Press, 1955), and his: *More Light on the Dead Sea Scrolls* (New York, Viking Press, 1958), superb volumes, delightfully written and conservative; F. F.

Bruce: *Second Thoughts on the Dead Sea Scrolls* (Grand Rapids, Eerdmans, 1956); and Charles T. Fritsch: *The Qumran Community, Its History and Scrolls* (New York, Macmillan, 1956).

OLD TESTAMENT HISTORY

The most widely-used history of Israel in seminaries today is *A History of Israel* by John Bright (Philadelphia, Westminster Press, 1959), brilliantly written by an authority, but embracing some liberal views. A more conservative work is *The Old Testament Speaks* by Professor Samuel J. Schultz, of Wheaton College (New York, Harpers, 1960).

BIBLE ATLASES

Remarkably, three truly great Bible Atlases were recently published within a ten month period (1956–1957). Of these three the greatest, *The Atlas of the Bible*, by L. H. Grollenberg (New York, Thomas Nelson, 1956), translated from a Dutch edition, contains 36 maps, 408 illustrations, approximately 75,000 words of text, and 3600 index entries. Though Grollenberg is a member of the Paulist Order, the work reveals no particular slant toward Catholic traditions, and is thoroughly conservative. The index is itself almost a dictionary of geographical terms, and the text states: "The principal purpose of this index is to catalog and describe all the geographical indications provided by the Bible. It, therefore, contains the name of every town and village, every mountain and valley, and every region, river, country and people which occurs in the Bible." In many ways, the best of contemporary

Bible atlases. (The Nelson Company has also issued, based on this work, *The Shorter Atlas of the Bible,* 2 maps, 200 plates.)

The famous map publishers, the Rand McNally Company, in the same year, published *The Rand McNally Bible Atlas,* edited and written by Emil Kraeling (Chicago, 1956), with 26 maps and 265 illustrations. The outstanding feature of this atlas is the text, approximately 235,000 words. Though the author takes the liberal and critical view of some texts, many of his pages describing the actual locations, e.g., of the various episodes in the life of David, the conquests of Solomon, etc., are the most authentic and up-to-date that we have. Here are some excellent discussions of the location of the crossing of the Red Sea, the geographical features of the life of Gideon, the archaeology of the life of Saul (20 pages), recent discoveries at Nazareth, the question of whether or not Paul visited Spain, and a chapter on a subject rarely treated, "The Geography of the Revelation."

Finally, there is the well-known *Westminster Historical Atlas to the Bible,* edited by Ernest Wright and Floyd V. Filson (rev. ed., Philadelphia, Westminster Press, 1955), which contains 30 maps, 110 illustrations, approximately 63,000 words of text, and more than 3100 geographical entries in the index. Some statements here, especially regarding the patriarchs, would not be acceptable to a conservative. There is no reference to the Tabernacle, nor does the word appear in the index, and there is a strange silence, as in other atlases, on the resurrection of Christ. It is, nevertheless, a standard work.[4]

The C. S. Hammond Company of New York has published *Atlas of the Bible Lands* at the low price of 50¢. The Fleming H. Revell Company has two pamphlets of maps, "An Atlas of the Life of Christ," and "An Atlas Illustrating the Acts of the Apostles and the Epistles."

BIBLICAL FLORA

The most important volume to be published in this century on Biblical flora is the result of years of study, *The Plants of the Bible,* by Harold N. Moldenke (Waltham, Mass., The Chronica Botanica Company, 1952), who recently retired as the Curator and Administrator of the Herbarium of the New York Botanical Gardens, an indispensable work, with full bibliographies.[5]

OLD AND NEW TESTAMENT INTRODUCTIONS

The most important conservative *Introduction to the Old Testament* is the one by Dr. Edward J. Young of Westminster Seminary, published by Eerdmans in 1949. For the New Testament, the most widely used of recent studies, is Alan H. McNeile's *Introduction to the Study of the New Testament* (rev. ed., Oxford, 1953). Then, of course, we have the thoroughly conservative *Introduction to the New Testament* by the late Dr. H. C. Thiessen, published by Eerdmans in 1944 but I cannot refrain from mentioning here the much older, but still invaluable work, by the late Dutch scholar, Theodor Zahn, *Introduction to the New Testament* (the 2nd edition, the English translation published by Scribners in 1917). This originally appeared in three volumes, but has since been published in a one-volume India paper edition.

No question is so frequently asked of the writer of this volume as, "What book shall I get for understanding the Bible?" Well, frankly, there is no one book, and never will be, which will tell us all we ought to know, and want to know, about the inexhaustible Word of God. More commentaries are now appearing than any one person will ever in his entire lifetime be able to read. In fact, during the last eight years, there have been launched in Great Britain and America, twenty-one different *series* of Bible Commentaries, some of which will extend to forty volumes. Among these are the *Annotated Bible Series* published by Harper; the new Revision of the *Cambridge Bible for Schools and Colleges*; and also revisions of the *Cambridge Greek Testament*, both published by Cambridge; The *Daily Study Bible*, issued in this country by the Westminster Press; the *Epworth Preacher's Commentary*, put out by the Epworth Press of London; the *Evangelical Bible Commentary*, projected by Zondervan; *Harper's New Testament Commentary*, which in Great Britain is known as *Black's New Testament Commentary*; the *Layman's Bible Commentary Series*, published by the John Knox Press, of Richmond; the *Shield Bible Study Series*, put out by Baker Book House, of Grand Rapids (inexpensive paper bound, but scholarly, works such as those by my friend, Gleason Archer, on Hebrews and Romans); the *Tyndale New Testament Commentaries*, issued by Eerdmans; and, of course, the huge *Interpreter's Bible*.

In the Roman Catholic Church, the Confraternity of Christian Doctrine of Patterson, New Jersey, is publishing a new series of commentaries; and the Jewish Publication Society of America is proposing a series on the Old Testament. I have purposely left to the last what, I think, is the most important of all these series, The *New International Commentary on the New Testament,* published by Eerdmans, certainly the most important work on this part of the Bible to appear in our generation. Among the volumes thus far published are those by Geldenhuys on Luke; F. F. Bruce on Acts. The work on Second Corinthians by Philip Hughes is in my opinion one of the most important commentaries on Paul's Epistles to be published in the last twenty years. (This series is published in London by the Inter-Varsity Christian Fellowship as the *New London Commentary.*)

COMMENTARIES ON THE ENTIRE BIBLE

While there has been a number of one-volume Bible commentaries published since the beginning of this century, I am thoroughly convinced that by far the most important is the monumental *New Bible Commentary* published in 1952 by the Inter-Varsity Christian Fellowship of London, with fifty contributors. This has excellent introductions to each book, and splendid excursi on matters relating to canonicity, eschatology, Biblical criticism, etc., a book for one's desk.

Inasmuch as I am writing for laymen, as well as ministers, and ministers who must preach every Lord's day, I hope I will be allowed to say a word here of the writings of Alexander Maclaren and Joseph Parker.

If one is devoting his life to preaching, then he certainly ought to have in his library that remarkable work by Dr. Alexander Maclaren, of Manchester, *Expositions of Holy Scripture*, which has appeared in various editions, the best one being that put out by Hodder and Stoughton, bound in 25 uniform volumes. The late Sir William Robertson Nicoll said of Maclaren: "In public his whole business was to expound the Word of God. All the wisdom of the world was to him contained in the Bible, but his business was to apply the Bible to life, and he read very widely in general literature. He was a close student of history and was not ignorant of science. He studied the living book of humanity. His whole effort was to bring Bible truth into effective contact with the human heart . . . He was clearly a man of genius and these are very rare. So long as preachers care to teach from the Scriptures they will find their best guide and help in him. It is difficult to believe that his Expositions of the Bible will be superseded. Will there ever again be such a combination of spiritual insight, of scholarship, of passion, of style, of keen intellectual power? We shall not see his like again. The generations to come will care little or nothing for our sermons for the times; but they will listen to the sweet, clear voice of the man who preached to the end of Gilead, and Beulah and the Gates of Day." Maclaren has been at my side now for nearly twenty years. Some pages at times have failed to yield much to my mind and heart, but that was probably due to my own stupid and dull nature; yet, twenty times out of twenty-one, I always find something helpful, if I read very long in these marvelous volumes. One cannot preach as

Maclaren wrote, but one will here find stimulating suggestions, and, quite embarrassing, he will have shown to him many things in the passage he plans to expound, that he would not have seen had he not read Maclaren.

The man who is devoting his life to expounding the Scriptures will also want the famous *People's Bible*, by Joseph Parker, for many years minister of the City Temple, in London. This work was published some years ago (without date) in this country in 28 volumes, the last volume being devoted entirely to an index. It is, for the most part, a collection of the expositions which Dr. Parker gave from year to year to the great throngs that gathered to hear him in London. There is no work quite like it. Some of its pages simply scintillate with brilliance, and at times the speaker soars into the very heights of inspired oratory, pressing home some great truth that has been burning in his heart for weeks, with tremendous power and effectiveness. Thus, e.g., the six pages (in the volume on Genesis) on "The Making of Man," expounding the last six verses of the first chapter of Genesis, I think could have been written by no other man in the English world of his time. I know some ministers who rather sneer at Parker's *People's Bible*, and think it is only for immature students and young preachers. Well, I will not contradict them with any words of my own, but may I call attention to two verdicts concerning this work and the author of it: Spurgeon said of Parker, "he condenses wonderfully, and throws a splendor of diction over all that he pours forth. He seems to say all that can be said on a passage. One is struck with his singular ability and special originality. He is a man of genius. His track is his own, and the jewels which he lets fall are from his own caskets; this will give a permanent value to his works, when the productions of copyists will be forgotten." Dr. Marcus Dods, an altogether different type than Spurgeon, said before the work was even finished, "The book is wholly and from the root Dr. Parker's own. Not an echo of any former commentary is to be heard in it. 'Genius,' said John Foster, 'is the gift of lighting one's own fire.' Dr. Parker is self-kindling."

Of course, a word must be said here about Matthew Henry. I cannot state, as some do, that I have read through the entire work. The great commentator, of course, lived at a time when the *historical* investigation of the Scriptures had hardly begun, and of course, was not acquainted with the results of Biblical archaeology. His commentary is distinctly devotional, and in this realm it will remain in the very first class, as long as the Christian Church is on earth. Spurgeon used it continuously. If it would help me to preach like Spurgeon, I would read in it for hours every day. However, I cannot with fairness insist that Bible students should have on their shelves any work which I myself have not found more or less indispensable. The work originally appeared in five volumes, London, 1708–1710, though Matthew Henry himself lived to complete it only as far as the end of the book of the Acts. (Since 1890 published in this country exclusively by Fleming H. Revell Company.) Whitefield read the work through four times, the last time on his knees.

It is a pleasure to state here that in 1960, there was brought out in London, and by Zondervan here, a one-volume edition of Matthew Henry's commentary by the late Dr. Leslie F. Church, on which the Editor had worked for years. All redundancies, duplications, etc., have been eliminated. Everything in these 2000 double column pages is in the words of Matthew Henry, not revisions of his paragraphs, a volume containing approximately three million words and this is all one will have time for in the middle of this twentieth century of Matthew Henry.

COMMENTARIES ON SOME INDIVIDUAL BOOKS

It will be impossible here to mention even one commentary on each of the books of the Bible. Today, unquestionably, the most important single volume on Genesis is by Professor H. C. Leupold (Columbus, Wartburg Press, 1942), a great and thoroughly conservative scholar, full of rich things, and I greatly regret that in three recent bibliographies for ministers issued by certain theological seminaries, this superb work is not even referred to. I am sure that many will still find value in the famous work on Genesis of the latter part of the nineteenth century, by Franz Delitzsch. In 1909, in the well-known *Devotional Commentary Series*, three volumes on Genesis appeared by Dr. W. H. Griffith Thomas. He had mastered all the relevant literature, and while the work is based on sound scholarship, it is truly devotional. A work, which many are not acquainted with, is *Hebrew Ideals—A Study of Genesis from Chapters XI-L*, (4th ed., Edinburgh, 1922). The author, Dr. James Strahan, was for years the Professor of Hebrew and Biblical Criticism in Magee College, Londonderry, England. Some of the chapter heads alone will give an indication of the rich things that are in this volume: "Separation," "Blessedness," "Worship," "Truth," "Decision," "Warfare," "Peace," "Assurance," "Hospitality," "Laughter," "Tears," "Farewell," "Faith."

The work by Chadwick on Exodus in the *Expositor's Bible* is a classic, so also is the volume by Kellogg on Leviticus in the same series. On Judges, the meatiest volume I have ever seen is one rarely come upon, *A Critical and Expository Commentary on the Book of Judges* (London, 1885), by A. R. Faussett of the famous Jamison, Faussett, and Brown Commentary. This is a masterpiece.

The great series by Keil and Delitzsch are well worth studying even now for the books of Samuel, Kings, and Chronicles. The three best volumes, I believe, on the book of Job would be the large *Commentary on the Book of Job* by Samuel Cox (London, 1880); the classic volume in the *Cambridge Bible for Schools and Colleges* by A. B. Davidson; and the beautifully written *The Book of Job*, by James Strahan (2nd ed., Edinburgh, 1914).

The two most important works on the Psalms, I would say, are *The Book of Psalms* by J. J. Stewart Perowne, first appearing in 1876, with a 5th edition, London, 1884, and then, of course, the standard work by A. F. Kirkpatrick, in the *Cambridge Bible for Schools and Colleges*. Maclaren's work on the Psalms in *The Expositor's Bible* has become famous. The seven-volume work by Charles H. Spurgeon, *The Treasury of David*, is sometimes sniffed at, but a real scholar like Dr. Philip Schaff did not hesitate to say: "The most important and practical work of the ages on the Psalter is *The Treasury of David* by

Charles H. Spurgeon. It is full of the force of the genius of this celebrated preacher, and rich in selections from the entire range of literature." On the book of Isaiah, one will still find great nuggets in the two volume commentary by the German scholar we have already referred to, Franz Delitzsch. The two volumes on Isaiah in the *Expositor's Bible* by George Adam Smith (New York, 1903), were acclaimed with fervor everywhere in the English world immediately upon its publication. His pages sparkle with brilliance, and are so suggestive that one preaching on the text he is commenting upon cannot get away from his remarks. On the other hand, the author's work here, as well as in his volumes on Jeremiah, and the Minor Prophets, is vitiated by his bondage to the theories of the higher critical school, and he does not mind chopping up the text whenever he feels so inclined. In reading Professor Smith, one must ever carry with him a discerning spirit, appropriating the gold and rejecting the tin.

There are a number of volumes that attempt to survey the prophetical writings of the Old Testament, among which, I would say, one of the best is by H. L. Ellison, *Men Spake From God* (London, the Paternoster Press, 1952). On the book of Daniel though I would not agree with all of his interpretations, there is nothing better than the notable work by Professor H. C. Leupold, whom I referred to above. For the latest scholarly approach to all the problems of Daniel, abreast of all the literature published up to that time, with some liberal conclusions indeed, is the well-known work by the late Professor James G. Montgomery in The International Critical Commentary series. I

mention this because the work must be consulted, but
never to be taken as final authority, for any one
holding conservative views of the Scriptures. In
1923, a volume was published in London, *In and
Around the Book of Daniel*, by Charles Boutflower,
which is principally valuable for its historical and
archaeological material, yet contains exceedingly rich
chapters on three or four of the most important prophecies in Daniel. In historical matters it is the finest
work of its kind in our language. I do not think that
in any other book e.g., one will come upon the real
meaning of the strange words written on the wall of
the great dining hall of Belshazzar's palace, the night
of Babylon's fall, so clearly explained. It concludes
with an excellent chapter on the testimony of Christ
to the book of Daniel.

A worthwhile volume is by Professor Edward J.
Young of Westminster Seminary, *The Prophecy of
Daniel*, though for one so firmly believing in inspiration as he, it is strange to find him refusing to believe
that the oft repeated chronological data of the famous
passage in chapter 9 is to be taken literally (Eerdmans, 1949).

On the Minor Prophets, there is still nothing to compare with the two volumes in the Keil and Delitzsch
series. Dr. Theo. Laetsch published a scholarly work,
The Minor Prophets, which is thoroughly conservative,
though his views of the return of Israel, and a number
of other prophecies, would not be my views at all
(Concordia, St. Louis, 1956). The same author did
a good work on Jeremiah in 1952. A small, but valuable, handbook is *The Twelve Minor Prophets* by the

late Dr. George L. Robinson, originally (1926, reprinted by Baker in 1952).

I have always felt myself that the greatest single volume on any *one* of the Minor Prophets is that truly searching study by David Baron, *The Visions and Prophecies of Zechariah* (3rd ed., London, 1919). This work, of some 570 pages, is the result of a profound knowledge of the Hebrew language and Hebrew thought, and a deep devotion to the Messiah. The general index itself occupies 24 columns, and, indicative of the richness of the exposition one discovers an index to Scripture passages alone of 17 columns!

The Gospels

As we approach the study of the Gospels, we will, of course, first of all, want to have a Harmony, and constantly use it. The one that has been at my right hand for years (I have worn out two copies), is that still standard work, *The Harmony of the Gospels for Historical Study,* by William A. Stevens and Ernest De Witt Burton, originally appearing in 1893 (4th ed., rev., New York, 1905). There is also a most helpful Harmony by the late Dr. Albert C. Wieand, for many years President of Bethel Biblical Seminary, entitled *Gospel Records of the Message and Mission of Jesus Christ,* a quarto sized work of some 260 pages (now published by Eerdmans). I have been told that when this appeared, it at once became the text book for the study of the Life of Christ in a number of courses on the New Testament in colleges in our country. Though it was written years ago, *The Introduction to the Study of the Gospels,* by Bishop B. F. Westcott is still recognized as a classic. Dr. W. Graham Scroggie has put an enormous amount of valuable material into his work, *A Guide to the Gospels* (London, Pickering and Inglis, 1948, 670 pages). Perhaps here should be mentioned the superbly valuable work by the distinguished authority on Palestine, Dr. Gustav Dalman, *Sacred Sites and Ways, Studies in the Topography of the Gospels* (New York, 1935). If I know anything of the literature relating to the records of our Lord's Nativity, I would say that the chapter in this book on Bethlehem contains more important, and in some places more new material, relating to this lovely town, than any chapter on the same subject that is available.

For commentaries on the entire New Testament, I would mention only four here. First of all, is the once indispensable work by Henry Alford, *The Testament for English Readers*, published in 1872 in four volumes, and still valuable. This is an abridgment of his larger four volume work, *The Greek Testament*. Then, of course, I cannot recommend too strongly the five volume *Expositor's Greek New Testament*, now published by Eerdmans. Some of the contributions here immediately won universal acclaim, such as Bruce on the Synoptics; Knowling on the Book of Acts; and Denney on Romans. (The pages on Revelation by Moffatt are bewilderingly worthless.) May I strongly commend the greatest series of commentaries on the New Testament written by an American scholar, the volumes by the late Professor R. C. H. Lenski, published by the Lutheran Book Concern of Columbus, Ohio. I have never failed to find help on any verse for which I needed assistance. I have used

Lenski more extensively in preparing *Peloubet's Notes* each year, than any other one author on both sides of the Atlantic. I do not see these scholarly, satisfying volumes mentioned in most bibliographies, which is not only not fair, but deprives the New Testament student of some of the most important works on these precious books appearing in modern times.

I cannot pass on to a discussion of commentaries on individual gospels without referring, for a moment, to a work which seems hardly to be known to Bible scholars today, and to which one almost never sees a reference, namely the *International Illustrated Commentary on the New Testament* in four quarto volumes, edited by no less a person than Dr. Philip Schaff, published by Scribners in 1890. I cannot speak with any intimate acquaintance on the value of the other contributions to this work but I do know that the treatment of the book of Revelation by Dr. William Milligan, who in addition to two other volumes on the book of Revelation, wrote the Commentary in the *Expositor's Bible* on this book, contains some of the most concise, penetrating paragraphs on almost all the basic passages of the Apocalypse that I have ever read.

One hardly knows where to begin in his recommendation on books on the Gospels. For brevity's sake, I must omit considerable bibliographic detail in naming some of these commentaries. On Matthew, the greatest work of a former generation, and still valuable, was the one by John C. Broadus. The volume by Alfred Plummer is also worthwhile, as well the extensive work by Lenski, of whom I have just spoken. I have always thought that the volume on Matthew by

G. Campbell Morgan was one of the finest things he ever did. On Mark, in addition to Lenski, and J. D. Jones in *The Devotional Commentary Series,* I cannot help but mention the monumental work on the Greek text of Mark by Swete. On the Gospel of Luke, a standard work is the volume by Alfred Plummer in *The International Critical Commentary* series. Then, on the Gospel of Luke, Morgan did a truly great work. (I have always thought his volumes on Mark and John were not up to his standard.) The best recent commentary is the one by Geldenhuys in Eerdman's *New International Commentary on the New Testament.* On the Gospel of John, there is a whole library of material. The most famous work on John, at the end of the last century, was by Westcott, and it is still worth consulting. A volume not too well known, but full of rich things, is the quarto sized commentary on this Gospel by the two distinguished Greek scholars, William Milligan and William F. Moulton (Edinburgh, 1898). Lenski has here done his very best in his *The Interpretation of St. John's Gospel,* a work of over 1400 pages. A very thorough and valuable piece of work is that by William Hendricksen, *The New Testament Commentary Exposition of the Gospel According to John* (Baker, Grand Rapids, 1953, 2 volumes). A volume now seldom seen, but very worthwhile, is *The Teaching of the Gospel of John* by the late Professor J. Ritchie Smith (New York, 1903). I cannot help but mention here two older works of John that will enrich the heart and mind of any student. First of all, there is the two volume commentary by F. Godet, for which additional notes were written by Timothy Dwight, then President of Yale

College (New York, 1886). From a theological standpoint, I have always felt that Godet was the preëminent work. Then, there is that classic treatment of John in the once widely used *Handbook for Bible Classes and Bible Students* by George Reith. Every sentence here counts. I felt, when I first read Reith's pages on Christ as the Lamb of God, that here was more wealth of material than could be found on hundreds of pages of sermons and ordinary commentaries on this subject.

Some Books on the Life and Teaching of the Lord Jesus Christ

I would judge that there are probably in English, and the languages of Western Europe, not less than 80,000 volumes relating to the person and work of Jesus Christ, perhaps more. Probably the one biography of Christ that has been more extensively used than any other in English, is the famous *Life and Times of Jesus the Messiah* by Dr. Alfred Edersheim, originally appearing in 1883, with an eighth edition as late as 1903. Edersheim, born in 1825, his death occurring in 1889, was of Jewish parentage, converted to Christianity while living in England, under the influence of a Scotch Presbyterian professor, John Duncan. Returning with him to Scotland, he studied theology at New College, Edinburgh, and at the University of Berlin, and at the age of 21 he was ordained a Presbyterian minister. In 1875 he became a clergyman of the Church of England, lecturing at Oxford University from 1884 to 1890. In some ways this book will probably never be surpassed, especially in showing the reader how Jewish customs of Christ's day, and contemporary Hebrew literature, illuminate the acts of our Lord and many of the teachings which were uttered by His holy lips. This work should be on the shelves of every Bible student who is seeking a real knowledge of the life of Christ as presented in the Gospels. Even such a higher critic as Driver said of it that it was "monument of learning, presented in an immediate readable form, and a storehouse of information on every subject which comes within its range." Let no minister think he is being economical by purchasing the abridged one-volume edition. If one has to wait a year, wait and get the two-volume edition, which is the only one which has all the virtues of this great work.

In 1862 Samuel J. Andrews published the first edition of his *The Life of Our Lord Upon the Earth Considered in Its Historical, Chronological and Geographical Relations.* Edition after edition was continually called for. In 1891 a new and wholly revised edition was issued, which stands even today as one of the most important single volumes on the life of Christ ever written. Stevens and Burton, in their *Harmony of the Gospels,* speak of this as "a work into which has gone a lifetime of scholarly research, and to which all students of the life of Christ are under large obligation." The late Professor Marcus Dods, who was as well acquainted with New Testament literature as probably any man of his day, and a famous author himself, in his preface to the great work on Christ by Lange, which we will shortly speak of, said of Andrews' volume, "This work is indispensable to any one who intends a thorough study of the subject, but yet has not access to the authorities themselves, or has not leisure to use them. The accuracy of his references, and impartiality of his citations, as well as the fairness and candor of his own judgments, inspire us with confidence in the author." Any remarks by us after two such commendations would be superfluous. I had the great privilege of writing a biographical introduction to a recent republication of this work by Zondervan.

In some ways the most monumental life of Christ that has been written in any language is the one by the famous commentator, John Peter Lange, published in English under the title, *The Life and Times of the Lord Jesus Christ* (Edinburgh, 1872, 4 volumes). The last two volumes were edited by Marcus Dods. These volumes are by one of the outstanding conservative theologians and New Testament scholars of that century in Germany, when Germany had many distinguished New Testament scholars. The work is profound, theological, tremendously suggestive, exhaustive, occasionally perhaps a little tedious, but never failing to move and inspire the careful reader, indeed, so much so, that one cannot read more than twenty or thirty pages of the work at a time. I have found, in referring to this work during the years, that comparatively few people in our country know of it, which leads me to lay added stress upon its greatness.

Thousands would agree, I believe, that the greatest single volume ever written by Dr. G. Campbell Morgan is his *Crises of the Christ* (Fleming H. Revell, 1903, and still in print). We have here really brilliant chapters on the Incarnation, the Baptism, the Temptation, the Transfiguration, the Crucifixion, the Resurrection, and the Ascension. I read this book first when I was about twenty years of age, and I must confess that no one volume has had since such an influence over my thinking, at least, as regards the Lord Jesus Christ. This is one of those books that a minister should secure on the very threshold of his life work. Morgan also did an excellent work on *The Teaching of Christ* (New York, 1913).

A. B. Bruce, *The Training of the Twelve*, first appeared in 1871, many editions followed, my own imprint reads 4th edition revised, and is without date. The late Dr. W. H. Griffith Thomas called it "one of the great books of the nineteenth century." There is nothing quite as important on the life of our Lord as related to the training of the twelve apostles as this volume. Now nearly a century old, it will still be found fresh and inspiring. Why has no book in seventy years been published on this theme to even stand alongside the volume by Bruce?

Of course, on the Parables and the Miracles, the volumes by R. C. Trench are still indispensable.[7] A great deal of literature has been published in the last few years on the Parables, of which I would like to recommend enthusiastically the searching study by G. H. Lang. (Grand Rapids, Eerdmans, 1958). Every minister should read with care the still important work, *The Divinity of Our Lord and Saviour Jesus Christ,* by Dr. H. P. Liddon, the Bampton Lectures for 1866, probably the greatest single work on the Deity of Christ ever composed. A classic, one of the best things he ever did, is Alexander Whyte's *The Walk, Conversation, and Character of Jesus Christ Our Lord,* now unfortunately out of print.[8] On the death of Christ, I would like, first of all, to

recommend a small handbook, if one might so desig-
nate it, *The Trial and Death of Jesus Christ,* by James
Stalker (London, 1894). This volume has chapters on
most of the characters participating in the great
events centering in our Lord's death, and chapters on
the Seven Words from the Cross, etc. Then, there is
that profoundly theological work by George Smeaton,
*The Doctrine of the Atonement as Taught by Jesus
Christ Himself.* This originally appeared nearly
one hundred years ago and has been republished
lately by Zondervan. The author was for many
years the Professor of Exegetical Theology at New
College, Edinburgh. In some ways, I believe, the
greatest single work on every aspect of the death of
Christ is still that classic work by Europe's greatest
preacher in the middle of the nineteenth century, *The
Suffering Saviour,* by F. W. Krummacher. This volume had become quite scarce until Moody Press began
its Wycliffe series and it was my privilege to write the
biographical introduction to this first of that series.
Should one wish to continue further study in this inexhaustible subject, then he should secure, and read
with care, the three volumes by the Dutch theologian,
K. Schilder, *Christ in His Sufferings* (1938); *Christ on
Trial* (1939); and *Christ Crucified* (1940), all of these
published by Eerdmans.

Some years ago, the late Professor Andrew M. Fairbairn, in the opening pages of his *Studies in the Life of
Christ* (1880), very forcefully spoke of the inexhausti-
bleness of the problems which relate to the person and
work of Jesus Christ, and perchance all my readers
have not seen these words, I trust they will bear with

me if I place the paragraph before them: "The greatest problems in the field of history centre in the Person and Life of Christ. Who He was, and what He was, how and why He came to be it, are questions that have not lost and will not lose their interest for us and for mankind. For the problems that centre in Jesus have this peculiarity: they are not individual, but general—concern not a person, but the world. How we are to judge Him is not simply a curious point for historical criticism, but a vital matter for religion. Jesus Christ is the most powerful spiritual force that ever operated for good on and in humanity. He is today what He has been for centuries—an object of reverence and love to the good, the cause of remorse and change, penitence and hope to the bad; of moral strength to the morally weak, of inspiration to the despondent, consolation to the desolate, and cheer to the dying. He has created the typical virtues and moral ambitions of civilized man; has been to the benevolent a motive to beneficence, to the selfish a persuasion to self-forgetful obedience; and has become the living ideal that has steadied and raised, awed and guided youth, braced and ennobled manhood, mellowed and beautified age. In Him the Christian ages have seen the manifest Good, the Eternal living in time, the Infinite within the limits of humanity; and their faith has glorified His sufferings into a sacrifice by the Creator for the creature, His death into an atonement for human sin. No other life has done such work, no other person been made to bear such transcendent and mysterious meanings. It is impossible to touch Jesus without touching millions of hearts now living and yet to live. He is whatever else He may be, as a world's imperishable wonder, a world's everlasting problem, as a pre-eminent object of human faith, a pre-eminent subject of human thought."

The Book of Acts

On the book of Acts, there are available now, two excellent studies by F. F. Bruce. There is his *Acts of the Apostles*, which is a commentary on the Greek text (London, Tyndale Press, 1952), and then his later work on Acts in the *New International Commentary on the New Testament*. Preëminent is the work I have just referred to above of R. J. Knowling in the *Expositor's Greek Testament*, and the best piece of *exposition* on Acts we have, in G. Campbell Morgan's *The Acts of the Apostles* (Fleming H. Revell, 1924). How many impressions have been issued of Sir William Ramsay's *St. Paul the Traveler and Roman Citizen*, first published in 1895, I do not know. Probably no one work on this subject has had so great an influence over the interpretation of the book of Acts since its publication as this work of Ramsay.

Though they may never be able to secure the volume, I want to call the attention of all students of the New Testament to a work by the famous missionary, T. Walker, simply entitled *The Acts of the Apostles*, originally appearing in *The Indian Church Commentary Series*, in 1910, published by S.P.C.K. in 1919. The author was a careful student of the Greek text, and he sees every line of the Book of Acts in the light of missionary approach. At the conclusion of the discussion of each chapter, he summarizes its teachings. The introduction is invaluable. I was introduced to this work by the late Mr. Fred Mitchell, of the China Inland Mission, though it took me eight years to find a copy for sale. I hope some publisher will undertake the reissuing of this precious volume.[9]

The Epistles of St. Paul

Charles Hodge: *A Commentary on the Epistle to the Romans* (new edition, revised, and in a great measure rewritten, New York, 1882), is a classic. The late Professor William Sanday spoke of this volume as "a satisfactory, well-limited doctrinal exposition, based on theprinciples of the Westminster Confession." The late Francis L. Patton called this Hodge's "greatest exegetical work and one of the most masterly commentaries on this Epistle that has ever been written." When one is studying the Epistle to the Romans, no matter what commentary he has on his shelf, if Hodge is there, he will soon learn to turn to it first. The reader should be warned against buying the abridged edition of this volume, for the massive qualities of this work do not re-appear in the abridged edition, and one almost wastes money in buying the smaller book.

Handley C. G. Moule: *The Epistle to the Romans* (originally published in the *Expositor's Bible*, 1893) has been blessed to thousands. Moule was a perfect combination of a great scholar and a great saint, which, incidentally, is a rare combination to come upon. Dr. Griffith Thomas, some years ago, said of this work: "It is no exaggeration to say that for a combination of profound scholarship and equally profound spirituality, this book on Romans is unequalled, and if any one can only afford to buy one book on this Epistle, let him by all means obtain this one." Moule does not take the place of Hodge, nor does Hodge take the place of Moule. There is more Calvinistic theology in Hodge, and there is more spiritual application of the great doctrines of Romans in Moule. Two other very valuable works on Romans, among the great number that could be mentioned, both of which will prove very helpful to the minister, are H. P. Liddon's *Explanatory Analysis of Saint Paul's Epistle to the Romans* (London, 1893), in which will often be found the finest English definitions of some of the more difficult words used by Paul to be discovered in any volume of New Testament interpretation; and the epochal work by Dr. William Sanday and Bishop Arthur C. Headlam, in the *International Critical Commentary* (1st edition, 1895, 2nd edition, 1896, latest imprint, New York, 1922), one of the most scholarly works on this Epistle in our language, marking a turning-point in the study of Romans in Great Britain and this country.

It will be impossible here to give a list of commentaries on each of Paul's epistles. The volumes in the *Expositor's Bible* by Moule, G. G. Findlay, and James Denney, are invaluable. Lightfoot's famous work on the Epistle to the Philippians, which went through twelve editions, needs no recommendation by me. Be sure to try to find a copy of the work on Colossians by Bishop W. R. Nicholson, *Oneness with Christ*. I have spoken on a former page regarding the great work on 2 Corinthians by Dr. Philip Hughes. In the wealth of material available for a study in the Pastoral Epistles, one should be sure to secure the volume in the *Devotional Commentary* series by Bishop Moule.

On the life and work of Paul, the famous two volume

Life and Epistles of St. Paul by W. J. Conybeare and
J. S. Howson, is still invaluable. If possible, secure
the large edition with steel engravings. James Stalker,
whose small work, *The Life of Saint Paul,* is easily
the most satisfactory work on this subject for its size,
enjoying an extensive circulation, says that the volumes by Conybeare and Howson "will probably always keep the foremost place; in many respects it is
really perfect; and a teacher who has mastered it will
be sufficiently equipped for his work and require no
other help." G. G. Findlay stated, a few years ago,
that this work is "the foundation of historical and
psychological study of Paul's work in England." Sir
William Ramsay is probably correct in the following
criticism: "Conybeare and Howson have attempted
in a most scholarly way to set forth a picture of the
situation in which Saint Paul found himself placed in
the cities of Asia and Galatia, but the necessary materials for their purpose did not exist, the country was
unknown, the maps were either a blank, or positively
wrong in regard to all but a very few points; and,
moreover, they were often deceived by Greek and
Roman analogies."

Passing by other works which are important, may I
mention briefly the English translation of the work
by Olaf Moe, *Paul, His Life and Work* (Minneapolis,
Augsburg Press, 1950). This volume of 600 pages
is easily the best of the modern Lives of the Apostle,
abreast of the latest scholarship. A volume now almost forgotten, is *St. Paul and His Companions,* by
E. Basil Redlich (London, Macmillan 1913); the great
value of this work is a veritable Dictionary of 99 men
and women mentioned in the New Testament in rela-

tion to the great ministry of the Apostle Paul. Each of these biographical sketches, not only presents all the Biblical material, but also gives full references to all the early traditions in post-apostolic literature to the characters that are therein mentioned. In this Dictionary is a three page discussion of "The Brother Whose Praise in the Gospel" of 2 Corinthians 8: 18, 19. There are separate chapters on St. Paul and Barnabas, the Ephesian Friends, the True and False Friends, etc.

The Epistle to the Hebrews

Probably the book most often recommended for the study of the Epistle to the Hebrews is the one by A. B. Davidson, for many years Professor of Hebrew at New College, Edinburgh. Then there is the work by Adolph Saphir: *The Epistle to the Hebrews, an Exposition* (n.d., many different editions, two volumes). Though Saphir provokes us at times by evading many of the difficult exegetical problems raised by this Epistle, and though he elaborates upon some less important matters, while severely abbreviating his exposition of some much greater matters, and though there are many repetitions in this book, still it is one of the finest expository works in our language, exceptionally rich from a devotional standpoint, and should stand on the shelves of every Bible student's library. B. F. Westcott has also done a monumental work, *The Epistle to the Hebrews, the Greek Text with Notes and Essays* (2nd edition, London, 1892). F. Delitzsch has given us a massive work on this Epistle in his *Commentary to the Hebrew Translated from the German Text* (Edinburgh, 2 volumes, 1887).

Perhaps Delitzsch's book is a greater work than the one by Davidson, but in this one place I am thinking of the virtues of the compactness and conciseness, and also remembering that many who will be reading these pages do not know Greek—the Davidson book requires no knowledge of Greek, but the Delitzsch work demands it. The most exhaustive work ever written on Hebrews is *The Exposition of the Epistle to the Hebrews with Preliminary Exercitations*, by that great Puritan divine, John Owen, which he published in 1680, and which has been frequently reprinted (the edition in my library being published in New York, bearing the date of 1854, in 7 volumes, pp. 3969). But who today has time to read 4000 pages on one New Testament book?

The Epistles of St. John

It is remarkable how many excellent works there are on the Epistles of St. John. First of all, for those who are interested in minute exegesis, there is the standard work by Bishop Westcott, *The Epistles of John with Notes and Essays* (2nd ed., London, 1886). This work is somewhat similar to Westcott's monumental volume on the English text of the Gospel of John, though this is a commentary on the Greek text, with invaluable supplementary notes on some of the most important doctrinal subjects touched upon in this Epistle, as, e.g., "The Fatherhood of God," "The Idea of Christ's Blood in the New Testament," "The Powers of Evil," "Saint John's Teaching on Creation," "On the Idea of Love," "Sin Unto Death," "The Idea of Life," and then three long essays on "The Two Empires: The Church and the World," "The Gospel of

Creation" (46 pages), and "The Relation of Christianity to Art" (44 pages).

Then there is the truly monumental volume, *The Epistle of John Expounded in a Series of Lectures*, by Robert S. Candlish (Edinburgh, 1866). Candlish was for years the brilliant Principal of the New College, and minister of Free St. George's Church in Edinburgh. These lectures go to the very depths of the truths set forth in this precious, inexhaustible, and not always easily understood Epistle of the Beloved Apostle. Some pages here seem to be almost perfect. The book will search one's heart, it will lift him up into new heights, where he will see with greater clearness than ever before some of the precious privileges and obligations of the child of God. It is a work to turn to frequently for inspiration and strength, whether one is studying in this particular Epistle at the time or not. The volume had become very scarce until Zondervan republished it, for which I had the privilege of writing an introduction.

Finally, there are the revealing pages of Robert Law's *The Tests of Life* (2nd ed., Edinburgh, 1909).

The Book of Revelation

It is difficult to know what to recommend for the book of Revelation. I still think there is value in the famous three volume work by J. A. Seiss, *The Apocalypse, A Series of Special Lectures on the Revelation of Jesus Christ*, originally published in 1869. One of the profoundest volumes that I know of is the work of Robert Govett *Lectures on the Apocalypse* (London, 1870). This volume is an abridgment of a four-volume work which Govett published under the pseudonym Mathettees in 1865, extending to over two thousand pages. I have always found Govett's abridged work remarkably satisfying. My own opinion is that he brings to his interpretation a more thorough knowledge of the Scriptures in their bearing on the last book of the Bible than any other writer of his generation.

If I were asked what one volume I would suggest for the lay-reader for an understanding of the book of Revelation, I would recommend the work by Walter Scott, *Exposition of the Revelation of Jesus Christ.* (This appeared originally at the beginning of our century, and has frequently been reprinted.) A work rarely referred to today, but one which I have found exceptionally valuable, is the *Annotations on the Revelation of St. John the Divine* in the *Lutheran Commentary* series, by the late Dr. R. F. Weidner, for years Professor of Systematic Theology in the Chicago Lutheran Theological Seminary (New York, 1900). On the Greek text of Revelation, there is nothing equal to *The Apocalypse of St. John* by Henry Barclay Swete (3rd ed., 1917). His knowledge of the meaning of the Greek words is unparalleled among interpreters of his day. He knows how to compress much in a small space. Swete often recognizes passages in the book of Revelation speaking of world convulsions, the upheaval of governments, universal war and violent opposition to God as marking the end of this age. In the volume on Revelation in the famous Lange series of commentaries, the notes by the American editor, E. R. Craven, make the volume doubly valuable (New York, 1874). A volume not too well known in this generation is the work by William Lee

in the *Anglican Commentary* edited by F. C. Cook
(New Testament, Volume IV, New York, 1890). This
is especially valuable because the author gives comprehensive surveys of the different interpretations of
a disputed passage. A work too rarely seen today is
The Doctrine of the Apocalypse by Hermann Geb-
hardt (English translation, Edinburgh, 1878). I must
not close this too brief list without referring to one of
the truly great works on prophecy of the nineteenth
century by a distinguished Swiss theologian, *The
Prophecies of Daniel and the Revelations of St. John,
Viewed in Their Mutual Relation* by Carl August
Auberlen (trans. by Adolph Saphir, Edinburgh, 1856).

While we are speaking of works on Revelation, may
I add that we are in great need of a comprehensive
work covering all the major subjects of biblical prophecy with adequate bibliographies. Until that volume
appears, we must be satisfied with less. Probably the
most comprehensive work thus far is *Things to Come*
by J. Dwight Pentecost (Findlay, Ohio, Dunham,
1958). My colleague, Dr. George Ladd, has written
two books that are widely read, and exercising considerable influence on both sides of the Atlantic, *The
Blessed Hope* and *The Gospel of the Kingdom* (both
published by Eerdmans).

THREE ADDITIONAL VOLUMES

Before concluding our discussion of literature pertaining to the New Testament, the following works, I
believe, will be found helpful. F. F. Bruce, *Are the
New Testament Documents Reliable?* (Eerdmans,
Grand Rapids, 1954); Ernest DeWitt Burton, *New

Testament Word Studies (Chicago, 1927) ; and W. E. Vine: *A Comprehensive Expository Dictionary of New Testament Words* in four volumes (London, Oliphants, 1940–1946).

SCIENCE AND THE BIBLE

In a day such as this, one cannot escape problems raised by modern science in relation to evolution. The best single volume, from a conservative standpoint, that has thus far appeared, is the work by Dr. Bernard Ramm, *The Christian View of Science and the Scriptures* (Eerdmans, Grand Rapids, 1954). The most important work on evolution in relation to the Christian faith is the one edited by Dr. Russell L. Mixter of Wheaton College, *Evolution and Christian Thought Today* (Eerdmans, Grand Rapids, 1959). This work is a volume of heavy reading, but eminently worthwhile. Two works of a more liberal character are E. L. Mascall, *Christian Theology and Modern Science* (London, Longman's Green, 1956), and John Dillenberger, *Protestant Thought and Natural Science* (Garden City, Doubleday, 1960), with an extensive bibliography.

A FEW ADDITIONAL WORKS

I never grow weary of recommending that great series of volumes, *Bible Characters* by Alexander Whyte. Whyte was the greatest preacher in Scotland in the last part of the nineteenth century. There was no one like him in his day, and there has been no one like him since. Probably the greatest work Whyte ever published is this series of lectures on Bible characters; there is nothing to compare with it in the

English language, and I doubt if there is in any language. Some of these chapters will send one weeping to one's knees; others will make one shudder; others will drive one into the pulpit to preach with new power, new conviction, and new fervor. No one could write the three pages that are to be found in the chapter on Belshazzar, on the phrase, "Thou art weighed in the balance and art found wanting," but Alexander Whyte. His account of Noah's shame and Ham's treachery should be read by every father and every son in America. What writing! What exaltation! What awful penetration into the wickedness of the human heart! What an apprehension of the horribleness of sin, and the wonders of God's mercy! What a revelation of the responsibility and the greatness of life lived in the will of God, and of the inevitable depravity that awaits the soul rebelling against God! I would almost say that the first books a man ought to have on his shelves are these six volumes. But not saying it about any one volume, I would not say it about this work of Whyte.

In 1864, the Bampton Lectures were delivered by T. D. Bernard, published that year, and in many subsequent editions *The Progress of Doctrine in the New Testament*. In this volume Dr. Bernard, in a learned, reverent, and truly fascinating way, presents the thesis that there is a perfect development of doctrine in the New Testament writings in the order of their canonical arrangement. "The four Gospels, the book of Acts, the collection of Epistles, and the Apocalypse, are regarded as severally exhibiting definite stages in the course of divine teaching, which have a natural fitness to succeed each other." Dr. Arthur T. Pierson called this "one of the grandest books of the century." Bishop Moule spoke of it as "that masterly book." Dr. G. Campbell Morgan stated, "A more valuable series of lectures was never delivered upon that great subject than these." The volume can be picked up second-hand at a very reasonable price, and its arguments will simply thrill any one interested in the Word of God.

In addition to the volumes I have already mentioned by Sir William Ramsay, I must say a word concerning his *The Bearing of Recent Discoveries on the Trustworthiness of the New Testament* (1914). Almost all of this volume is devoted to a discussion of the major historical character and episodes in the Book of Acts. One might speak of this as the harvest of years in the author's constant, indefatigable, scholarly investigation of the great historical problems of the New Testament. Probably no one book has appeared in English presenting such overwhelming evidence for the historical trusworthiness of the writings of St. Luke as this volume. Some of its discussions seem to be almost final and perfect. In consulting this great work by Ramsay the other day, my eye fell upon a sentence which, though I had read it twenty years ago, had entirely passed out of my memory. The sentence needs no comment, but more than one truth can be discovered in its words: "my mother's love for Paul began to move in my mind; and she and I read together Conybeare and Howson's Life and Translation of the Letters."

A small volume, which I regret is out of print, will prove of infinite help to those who are asked the question as to whether there were any testimonies in early pagan literature to the person of Christ. This is a volume by C. R. Haines, which has for its full title, *Heathen Contact with Christianity During its First Century and a Half*. Haines gives us first the original Greek and Latin text with full references, from the pagan authors, and, on the opposite page, the English translations of these extracts, together with an Introduction of thirty pages (Cambridge, 1923).

A most interesting volume, with some truly profound articles, is *A Companion to the Bible* by J. J. Von Allmen as the general editor, who is the Professor in the Theological Faculty of the University of Neuchatel (New York, Oxford University Press, 1958). This is a volume arranged in Dictionary order with excellent discussions of such subjects as Adoption, the Advent, the Ages, Conscience, Covenants, etc., etc. As an illustration of the method pursued, there is an article simply entitled "Names—Geographical." Here is a discussion of the Fertile Crescent, of the deeper meanings of Babylon, the Significance of the Wilderness in the Life of Israel, the Meaning of Jerusalem, etc. This book needs to be read carefully, rather than consulted from time to time.

A work for advanced students, with thorough bibliographic references to Hebrew, Greek, and Latin Lexicons, and modern German and French literature, is *Multi-Purpose Tools for Bible Study*, by Frederick W. Danker (St. Louis, Concordia Publishing House, 1960). Here are interesting discussions on the Nestle Text, the History of the Septuagint, the Use of the Septuagint, the Dead Sea Scrolls, and an excellent concluding chapter on Commentaries. This volume is written particularly for those who are devoting their

lives to Bible study, especially those who will be working in the original languages. The author frequently
shows how to use lexicons and concordances, e.g., in
the study of a given text, such as Luke 16: 19–31.
This is the finest work of its kind available today;
written with fervor and full knowledge. Its discussions include far more of the continental works than
do those of earlier attempts. This is a "must" for
advanced Bible students.

I think here I would do my readers a favor if I
called their attention to a work that has not yet received the notice which it deserves. I am referring to
Jerome's Commentary on Daniel (Grand Rapids,
Baker Book House, 1958), which is the first translation
to appear in English of Jerome's Latin commentary on
Daniel, easily the most important commentary on
Daniel down to the time of the Reformation. This
work has been superbly done by my scholarly colleague, Dr. Gleason L. Archer.

I cannot let such a bibliographic list as this appear without mentioning a recent work which is
being deservedly praised on both sides of the Atlantic, *Studies in the Sermon on the Mount,* by Dr. D.
Martyn-Lloyd Jones of Westminster Chapel, London,
probably the most influential non-conformist preacher
in England today. (Grand Rapids, Eerdmans, 2 volumes, 1959–1960). I have been reading books on the
Sermon on the Mount now for thirty years in preparation for *Peloubet's Notes* and it would be my opinion
that this is the most penetrating, satisfying study of
this great discourse that has been published during the
twentieth century.

Most pastors, and teachers in Bible Institutes, will

sooner or later be asked questions about what is erroneously advertised as "The Lost Books of the New Testament," etc., and about the so-called "Acts of Pilate," etc. The best single help, a result of genuine scholarship, is that standard edition of all these uninspired documents, by the late learned M. J. Jones *The Apocryphal New Testament, being the Apocryphal Gospels, Acts, Epistles, and Apocalypse.* This work of 600 pages was first published by the Oxford University Press in 1924 and re-issued in 1945.

There is a volume, long out of print, and I regret quite difficult to secure, the contents of which need to be known to Christian students everywhere in this age of declining faith and the almost total unbelief of our leading scientists. I am referring to a work published in London by S.P.C.K. in 1913, *Modern Rationalism as Seen in Its Biographies,* by the late Canon Henry Lewis. This is a carefully documented study with a full apparatus of references, showing a thorough acquaintance with the original sources of the tragic consequences of rationalism in the lives of Voltaire, Thomas Paine, John Stuart Mill, Renan, Bradlaugh, Herbert Spencer, and Nietzsche, with briefer discussions of Goethe, Shelly etc., with a chapter on "Agnosticism and the Experiences which Death Brings."

There are two series of volumes that I am sure will be of great help to Bible students, though they belong to a former generation. First of all, there is the famous series, *Living Messages of the Books of the Bible,* by G. Campbell Morgan (first appearing in 1912, and often reprinted, in either two or three volumes). Then may I recommend strongly the works by William G. Moorehead, e.g., *Outline Studies in the Books of the Old Testament,* etc. Dr. Moorehead gives a short synopsis of each book, setting forth its principal theme, and then briefly expounds each major section in paragraphs crowded with the results of years of Bible study. One of the commendable virtues, especially of the New Testament studies, is his thorough wrestling with some major serious problems in the book. The greatest lexicon on the New Testament, in six quarto volumes, is the work by Kittel, in German. A number of the words in this exhaustive work have been translated into English and published in separate small volumes. Now Macmillan of Toronto has brought these together in three substantial volumes, embracing Kittel's treatment of such words as Love, Church, Sin, the Spirit of God, Faith, Gnosis, etc.

In 1884, a large work of over 2100 pages in three massive volumes was published by George N. H. Peters, *The Theocratic Kingdom of Our Lord Jesus Christ,* the most exhaustive work on prophecy ever produced by an American. In my last edition of *Profitable Bible Study,* I mentioned the fact that I had not been able to secure a copy of this then rare set of books, but I am very glad to report that since then, Kregel has reprinted these volumes (their first edition, in spite of its cost, was exhausted, and a second edition was soon called for). I had the privilege of writing an extensive biographical sketch of Mr. Peters for these two editions.

Evangelical students of the Bible and theology are now fortunate to have the excellent *Baker's Dictionary of Theology* edited by Dr. Everett F. Harrison with

Professor Geoffrey W. Bromiley as the associate
(Grand Rapids, 1960). One hundred twenty theologians and Biblical scholars in the English world
have made contributions to this now indispensable
work. Most of the articles are accompanied by helpful bibliographies. This is one of those few books that
any serious Bible student will continually want within
arm's reach of his desk.

I must not attempt to give even a brief bibliography
in the area of Church History, but I do believe two or
three titles of a basic significance should be mentioned
here. First of all, there is the epochal, really indispensable *Oxford Dictionary of the Christian
Church,* edited by F. L. Cross (Oxford University
Press, 1957). This volume of 1500 double column
pages is the indispensable one volume work of its kind
now available in our language, with standard articles
on every conceivable subject, and personality, of any
importance in these nineteen centuries of church history, even with articles on the books of the Bible. All
of these articles carry excellent separate bibliographies.

For those who are interested in the early development of doctrine, while a great many volumes could
be referred to, I especially would call attention to two
works by J. N. D. Kelly, *Early Christian Creeds,*
(London, Longman's Green, 1950), and *Early Christian Doctrines* (London, Adam and Charles Black,
1958). These volumes are the result of ripe scholarship and vast reading, and will introduce one to the
entire literature of these subjects.

I simply must here recommend, with great earnestness, a work I wish every Protestant minister in North
America would possess and read. This is *The History*

of Preaching in Britain and America by F. R. Webber
(3 volumes, Milwaukee, Northwestern Publishing
Company, 1952–1957, approximately 2100 pages). A
work such as this can only be written after a lifetime
of careful research. There are a number of names
here of preachers whose printed sermons were once
sold by the thousands of copies, whose names are now
forgotten, as well as careful studies of those outstanding men whose names are still remembered. Best of
all, the author is a conservative, who believes that
preaching should center in Jesus Christ, deriving from
the Word of God, and his judgments are the result of
that kind of a conviction.

CALVIN AND LUTHER

Of course, the two greatest commentators of the
Reformation on the Holy Scriptures were John Calvin and Martin Luther, and their works continue to
prove inexhaustible treasure houses of Biblical interpretation. A most extensive set of Calvin's commentaries in English was published by T & T Clark (1843–
1855 in fifty-one volumes). Eerdmans republished
this series in forty-five volumes in 1950. Some of
these volumes are now out of print. An entirely new
series is now being edited by Professor Torrance to appear in thirty volumes, of which some ten have already been published. Always remember, that while
Calvin was the greatest expositor of his day, he was
notably weak in many areas of Eschatology, which he,
no doubt, knew, and for that reason, he refrained from
writing a commentary on the Book of Revelation.

All of the major writings of Martin Luther are now,

at last, to appear in one uniform series of translations into English, a joint project by the Muhlenburg Press and Concordia, planned to extend to fifty-one volumes, of which a number have already appeared.

Professor Andrew Martin Fairbairn in the *Cambridge Modern History* has not spoken with exaggeration when he says of Calvin, "Modern oratory may be said to begin with him, and indeed to be his creation. He helped to make the vernacular tongues of Western Europe literary. He is the sanest of commentators, the most skilled of exegetes, the most reasonable of critics. His exegesis is never forced or fantastic; he is less rash and subjective in his judgments than Luther, more reverent to Scripture, more faithful to history, more modern in spirit." The Calvin Translation Society published all of Calvin's commentaries in the first decade of the second half of the 19th century, but of course in the passing of a century the set has become quite scarce. In the last three years we are greatly indebted to the William B. Eerdmans Publishing Company of Grand Rapids for republishing the entire series, in forty volumes, with an Introduction by various professors in America and Great Britain. It was my own great privilege to write the Introduction for the two volumes on Daniel. Calvin is weak in one area, and that is the field of predictive prophecy, as his book on Daniel will show, but he is superior to everyone else in the Reformation, and many commentators since the Reformation in getting at the historical meaning and spiritual essence of a text. As an illustration, his eight-page comment on Daniel's refusal to eat of the food set before him from

Nebuchadnezzar's table not only has never been equalled, but could never be equalled, I think, by any writer of modern times. He directs his thoughts continually to Christ. He had a vast knowledge of Greek and Hebrew and history, and, above all, he had a rich experience as a disciple of the risen Lord. He suffered persecution; he was a teacher and an administrator; he knew the relationship of religion to political life and to government; and he knew men. One may easily say that Calvin's series of commentaries is the greatest that has ever come from the pen of one man; others have surpassed him in certain areas of Biblical interpretation; others have since written more important commentaries on portions of the Word of God, but no *one* will probably ever again produce such an inexhaustible and perennially precious work as the ones that the great reformer wrote.

I would strongly commend to all Bible students that great work on the resurrection of Christ by the late W. J. Sparrow-Simpson, *The Resurrection and Modern Thought* (London, 1911). Among all the many good works on this subject, Simpson still stands before them all.

I am very glad to close this list of books with the title of a work which has come off the press the very week I am writing this chapter, a volume I had the privilege of reading in manuscript form and for which I had the honor of writing an Introduction. I refer to a much-needed work in the field of Biblical interpretation. Inasmuch as my entire volume deals with the study and interpretation of the Scriptures, it is fitting that it should conclude with a reference to a work which ought to be in the hands of all who intend to do serious work along this line. It is Dr. Bernard Ramm's *Protestant Biblical Interpretation,* published by the W. A. Wilde Company of Boston (1950, pp. xii, 197).

FOOTNOTES

[1] As as indication of the vastness of new works being contually published relating to the Bible and the Lord Jesus Christ, in *The Cumulative Book Index, 1953–1956,* there are under the words Bible, Jesus Christ, the Holy Spirit, the Lord's Supper, Prophets, Theology, etc., over 1400 different titles excluding all the titles that relate only to various editions of the Bible, and parts of the Bible, and versions. As another illustration, the *Journal of the Bible and Religion* for January, 1960, is an index to the last twenty-five volumes of this quarterly, and in the Index of Book Reviews, there are over 3100 titles —books that it was thought were worth reviewing and it did not contain all the important books in these subjects.

[2] Thinking that perhaps my readers might like to have a few biographical items concerning Dr. Young, who spent so many years on this concordance, let me summarize here the data found in the sketch of him, appearing in *The Dictionary of National Biography.* Robert Young was born in 1822, the son of George Young, a manager of a flour mill, in Haddingtonshire. After being educated in private schools, he was at the age of sixteen apprenticed to the printing business, and when twenty-five years of age established a printing shop and bookstore of his own. While learning the printing business, he devoted his spare time to the study of Hebrew and other oriental languages, at the same time zealously laboring in the great work carried on in the Sunday school of Dr. Chalmer's Territorial Church in West Port, Edinburgh. From 1856 to 1861, he was literature missionary and superintendent of the mission press at Surat. From 1864 to 1874 he conducted the "Missionary Institute"; in 1867 he made an extensive visit to the more important cities of our own country. It was in 1879 that he first brought forth his *Analytical Concordance to the Bible.* Most of his years were spent in Edinburgh where he died October 14, 1888. There is an exhaustive list of Young's grammatical and expository work in the *Encyclopedia of Liv-*

ing Divines by Philip Schaff and James Macauley Jackson (New York, 1890, pp. 247, 248).

[3] The (so it seems to me) fascinating subject of Bible Dictionaries has never been thoroughly investigated, and could easily become the subject of a worthwhile thesis for a doctorate. The most extensive list of Biblical and theological dictionaries published in our language is one that I constructed, appearing in the Library Bulletin of Fuller Theological Seminary, October, 1953—September 1954. I also have a chapter on this in my *Treasury of Books for Bible Study,* pages 98–113 (Natick, Massachusetts, W. A. Wilde, 1960).

[4] For a more extended discussion of recent Bible Atlases, see the book referred to in the previous note, pages 187–200.

[5] For a survey of the entire literature of books relating to Biblical flora, there is a chapter on this in the volume mentioned in the previous note, pages 71–87.

[6] May I call my reader's attention to an item relating to Mr. Parker, which I think not many of this generation are aware of. These are Parker's own words spoken in City Temple, London, on Sunday morning, following the death of Mr. Moody. "I notice that the Christian pulpit has suffered a severe loss within the last few days by the withdrawal from these grey scenes of time of Dwight Lyman Moody, known to all the Christian Church as a devoted, faithful, and successful evangelist. Mr. Moody was a stronger, capable man. Like a wise man, he knew his limitations, and he worked within them; he never wanted to be somebody else, it was enough that he knew his talent, whether one or two or five, and with wholeheartedness he gave himself to the highest of all work. There was a time when I was slightly disinclined to have much commerce or communion with Mr. Moody because I feared he was a man with only one set of sympathies. When I met him in his own house in America that feeling was instantaneously and completely dissipated; I found he was a big man, a man of wide views and wide sympathies, and that he only needed more light, in order thoroughly to enter into his privileges. He was pre-eminently, within his own limits, a preacher. Do not be misled by the word preacher, because it admits of several definitions, or, perhaps, many definitions have been unduly thrust upon it. I could not imagine Mr. Moody taking out of his satchel or pocket an elaborate essay which he was going to read to a stupefied and bewildered audience. He spoke right out of his heart, and grammar had sometimes to take care of itself, and logic had sometimes to get out of the way. But it was the Gospel Mr. Moody preached, a living, comprehensive, divine, everlasting Gospel. What is that Gospel but a

great welcome to the human heart to come to the living Christ and receive the assurances of pardon and growth and happiest destiny?

"Having a little feeling of hesitation as to whether he and I lived under the same firmament so far as theological views were concerned, I did not hasten to his house. Feeling that I was loitering by the way, he came to fetch me; that was extremely and beautifully Moody-like. He had a good deal of the disciplinarian and even of the soldier in his constitution. So he came to the hotel, about a mile away from his house, and said I must come at once. We all went with him. It was a simple, homely, comfortable, farm-like home on the hillside, a room on the right hand and a room on the left, and both the rooms and the passage included, some of us could put into one of our London houses. Mr. Moody beckoned me into a little room which he called his study, and taking two books out of his shelves he said, 'Look at these.' I looked at them. 'Open them,' he said. I opened them, and I found marks, notes, special indications of careful perusal; little sentences were marked that I should have thought Mr. Moody would have never noticed. And then said he to me, putting back these two volumes of *The People's Bible* into his shelves, 'I never travel without these, and these books have done more for me than any other books of the kind I ever read.' After that I could not suspect him of any tendency toward narrowness or exclusiveness, because I know that in *The People's Bible* there is room for everybody who is earnest in spirit and lovingly waiting for the consolation of Israel." (*The City Temple Pulpit*, Volume II, 1900, pp. 268-270).

[7] The *Notes on the Parables of Our Lord* first appeared in 1841, and his *Notes on the Miracles of Our Lord* in 1846. The first of these volumes reached its fifteenth edition in 1886, and the second one, a thirteenth edition in 1886.

[8] I hope every minister who might read these pages has in his own library that epochal soul-stirring biography of Dr. Whyte by G. F. Barbour, published in 1923.

[9] See Amy Carmichael: *This One Thing. Story of Walker of Tinnerelly* (Oliphants, London, 1950).

For those interested in more extensive bibliographies, may I suggest two of them. In 1960, Princeton Theological Seminary issued a *Bibliography for Bible Study for Theological Students*, extending to something over one hundred pages with perhaps 1500 titles, with bibliographic details. In 1961, the Inter-Varsity Fellowship of London published a revised edition of their valuable *Guide to Christian Reading*, which I would judge lists about 2,000 titles, conveniently classified and in many cases with the prices of books that are in print and an index of American publishers. This would be a more conservative list than the one published at Princeton.

In my *Treasury of Books for Bible Study*, in addition to the two chapters mentioned above, I have chapters giving bibliographic details in the History of Preaching, the Birth of Christ, the Virgin Mary, and Great Bible Dictionaries.

INDEX

163

Bill Prince